To be haunted is to glimpse a truth that
might best be hidden.
James Herbert

Also From Robert W. Parker

Louisville Ghost Walks
Haunted Louisville (2007)
Haunted Louisville 2: Beyond Downtown (2010)
Haunted Louisville 3: You Are Never Alone (2014)

Acknowledgements:

I'd like to recognize two dear friends who devoted a lot of time over the past four years with the work of this written project of *Haunted Louisville 4.... Dark Screams from Troubling Tales*, Lonnie and Roberta Brown, authors and ghost investigators in Louisville, Kentucky. The Browns have a combined total of 12 books over their writing careers, yet they have always had time to proofread, consult, offer advice and edit every story, not once, not twice, but sometimes, three times to ensure accuracy, suspense, and clarity of each story being told for the reader. Without their help and support, this book wouldn't have been possible. Please enjoy!

HAUNTED LOUISVILLE

4

DARK SCREAMS & TROUBLING TALES

An American Hauntings Ink Book

Original Cover Artwork Designed by

© Copyright 2019 by April Slaughter & Troy Taylor

Original Photographs by Robert W. Parker
Editing by Lonnie & Roberta Mae Brown

This Book is Published By:
American Hauntings Ink
Jacksonville, Illinois
http://americanhauntingsink.com

First Edition – July 2019
ISBN: 978-7324079-5-4

Printed in the United States of America

TABLE OF CONTENTS

A Ghost, Murder, and Mayhem in the Palace Theater's Alley

Some stories are easier to write than others. Some people I've been able to interview and hear their story. This isn't the case here, because I knew the victim who died a violent death, and the man who committed the murder. Some people, I've been acquainted with and I know their story, firsthand. This is that story.

I like to be involved in community affairs and events. One of my desires for helping others is my work with the homeless men and women in the city. One night a week, I and another companion, Cathy Smith, go out on the homeless mission route, seeking out homeless individuals and provide them with food, water, bedding, and personal contact with these folks. One of my homeless men that I provided care for, called home, the alley way behind the Palace Theater and 4th Street. He was Fredrick Baker. I don't exactly know Fred's story of how and why he became homeless, but I do know that he at one time, worked at the Brown Theater on Broadway as a stagehand. The good employees at

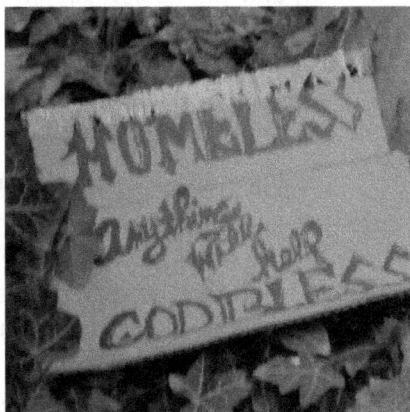

A cardboard sign found in the alley that was once the home for Freddy.

the Palace Theater would often check up on him, and provide him with handouts of food, water, and companionship. Then came one hot July day in 2015, when the homeless man, just wasn't there.

With my ghost story tours, I conclude at the Seelbach Hotel. Over my years there, I've gotten acquainted with several of the employees, mostly the doormen and valets. Before and after the tours, I'll talk to the guys, and always thank them for making my guests feel welcome inside of the hotel.

This is the location where I became acquainted with one of the doormen, Christopher Winstead II. Christopher is a 21-year-old Louisville resident who worked at the Seelbach Hotel, but he wasn't employed by the hotel. He worked for the car valet service that had the contract with the hotel.

I never suspected anything unusual, threatening or menacing about Christopher. Maybe I hadn't known him long enough, or maybe that's how he wanted everyone to perceive him. Unfortunately, Christopher had a dark, sinister side, that today, still chills me to the bone when I think about this episode and tell this story.

According to the media reports on the story and investigation by the local police department, Christopher drove around the streets of downtown and Old Louisville, 'looking for a victim.' He was about to call it a night and go home on this rainy evening, when he saw poor old Freddy Baker at a downtown gas station, on First Street, adjacent to I-65.

"It just kinda came on like a lightbulb," said Christopher in his phone call to his friend, Noah, who lives in New Jersey.

"I don't regret it," Christopher told Noah about the brutal slaying. "It doesn't ever keep me up at night or anything."

At the conclusion of the telephone call between Chris and Noah, Chris told Noah that he didn't have to worry, that he wasn't going to kill him! Noah was so disturbed and haunted by the chilling tale he had just heard, that he contacted Louisville Metro Police.

Let the local police investigate this murder, and maybe, just maybe, this was one of Chris' wild stories, Noah thought to himself. Louisville Metro Police took Noah's phone call seriously and sent homicide detectives to the location of Blevin's Gap Road, to search for the man who was reportedly, stabbed to death.

In early July 2015, Christopher found out what it was like to kill someone, and Freddy Baker, met up with an untimely death.

Noah recounted this conversation of the phone call that Christopher had told him.

"Christopher had just gotten off of work from his day shift at the Seelbach Hotel. It was a rainy, steamy summer night, and Christopher ran into Freddy at the gas station.

"Christopher offered the homeless Freddy Baker $50 if he'd help him move a dryer. That was the best scheme he could come up with at the time, and it worked.

"Freddy got into the car and agreed to help him to move it, which he thought was an easily way to earn an easy $50 bucks.

"Christopher drove Freddy out to his grandparents' home, out in the county, not far from Blevin's Gap Road.

"The car arrived out in the wooded area of the forest. They got out of the car, and Christopher had a hammer in the back of the car.

"Christopher knocked him unconscious from behind, with the force of the hammer, hitting Freddy in the skull. As Freddy's body staggered about from the impact, Christopher got his hunting knife and went to town on him."

"Christopher must have stabbed him, 17, 19 times, it just went so fast, the blood was flying and the body, just fell over, almost in a slow-motion style, until he landed at Christopher's feet.

"Using the toe of his boot, Christopher pushed over Freddy's lifeless body, and with the force of his foot pressed down upon the body, blood just oozed out of all the open wounds.

"Christopher's shirt was splattered in blood, and the hunting knife was covered in blood. Even blood from Freddy's body, had reached and dribbled down to Christopher's elbow.

"Not feeling remorse or anything, Christopher removed his shirt and balled it up, with the hunting knife inside. He then, tossed it into the trunk of his car.

"Christopher got into his car, and drove back to his home, and went to sleep. The next day, it was business as usual, and back to work at the hotel.

"Christopher said, 'I know I shouldn't have killed Baker and that it wasn't a smart thing to do, but he said he had cancer and didn't have much to live for anyway.'

"He continued on the phone, 'I'm not gonna say I'm not gonna kill again, but maybe if there is a next time, I would like it to be a little more planned out.'

"Christopher said he still had his bloodied clothes from the attack and the knife at his home. I'm 99.9% sure I will never be caught," he confided in his friend, Noah.

"Christopher reassured me, that I would remain safe," said Noah.

Louisville Metro Police paid Noah a visit in New Jersey. Using a recording device, Noah called Christopher, and engaged him into the conversation of the murder of Freddy Baker.

Christopher Winstead was arrested the day of that recorded phone call without incident.

It was several days before this grisly crime hit the news media, and several more days had passed before I had made any contact with the employees of the Palace Theater.

I was back on my Thursday night homeless route with my helpmate, Cathy Smith. We'd make our usual stops and then, cruise by the alley campsite of Freddy Baker. But Freddy wasn't there; he wasn't to be found. Neither Cathy Smith nor I thought anything too suspicious, and the last thing we thought was foul play. It's not unusual for homeless people to disappear for a few days or a few weeks, for any number of reasons. Sometimes, homeless people check into rehab centers, or become ill and are hospitalized, and sometimes, they are arrested and are in jail.

On the nights of my ghost walks, I always walk past the Palace Theater. In the months of July and August, the Palace Theater shows the classic movie series. The employees stand out front and greet their guests. The employees know me, and I know them, so we have a business relationship.

I would ask the employees, if they'd seen Freddy, and unfortunately, they would respond with no. The employees were worried as well. Freddy's things were still tucked away in cubby holes along the alley that he called home, totally undisturbed. I'd add that I've not seen him either, and I was looking for him.

Then, the horrible story hit the newspapers and the media! On one Friday night, I hurried to the Palace, hoping I'd see the employees. Those guys were waiting for me to come by as well. It was almost like, we both wanted to speak at the same time, when the feared question was spoken, "Have you seen the news about Freddy?"

"Yes, I saw it on the news and read the article in the newspaper. That was a horrible story, and what makes it worse is that I knew the valet from the Seelbach Hotel" I said.

"Hey, but did you know, several of us saw Freddy's ghost! We didn't know Freddy was dead.... But his ghost appeared in the alley. It was just as always! There he was! His ghost was there, and we didn't know he had been murdered!"

"How did Freddy look? Did he look like he'd been killed?" I asked.

"No, Freddy looked the same, just as he always did, like the same homeless guy that we'd seen many times before. He wasn't bloody or hurt or anything. But he never came close to us, we only saw him at a distance, which wasn't really like him. He'd approach us; he'd come down to talk with us, but on this day, he just remained at a distance. He wasn't pale or ghostly looking at all.

"It did turn out, that he was ghostly, because he was dead," exclaimed one of the employees. His eyes had a sad look to them, he looked like he was hurting emotionally, or troubled by something. He was always sociable with us, but when we saw him, he looked at us from a distance. We started walking down the alley toward him, but as we walked, he just kinda stepped backwards, keeping a distance from us, moving away.

"Apparently, Freddy didn't want conversation, or to be seen, but we didn't really know what was going on. A short time later, I opened up one of the back doors to the Palace to look for Freddy.

"I had stepped out back a few minutes later, and I looked to the left and saw him, then within seconds of turning around and doing what I needed to do, he was gone. Now that did surprise me, he was there but he'd just vanished within seconds."

A day later, it then, hit the news.

"By then, the news of his bloody murder had made the news, and we just stood looking at each other in disbelief, knowing, we'd seen his ghost and it was haunting the back side of the Palace Theater," commented one of the Palace Theater employees to me.

"Freddy liked it here, we'd show him some kindness, offer him some food and check in with him to see how he was doing. It would be only natural for his ghost to return to this location.

"We can't say for sure, but at least he might be about to have the 'rest in peace' for once in his life."

Author's Note: In December of 2017, the court charged Christopher Winstead with the kidnapping and murder of Frederick Baker. He was sentenced to 30 years in prison.

Art Eatables on Fourth with Bourbon, Chocolate and Ghosts

The bourbon infused chocolate candy shop on Fourth Street has occupied the Theater Building storefront for about four years. Little did the owners, Kelly and Forest, realize that their new business shop that is full of luscious chocolate and Kentucky bourbons, would come with a ghost.

I spoke with Kelly, the owner and one of her employees named Stacy. Both women are believers in ghosts and firmly believe that their store is haunted.

They even have named their ghost 'Fred.'

"What makes you think it is haunted?" I asked Kelly.

Kelly spoke up and said, "It wasn't long, once we'd set up business, that strange things would start happening. None of the guys ever experience anything, only the gals.

A chocolate and bourbon loving Ghost! Most definitely!

"For one thing, I'd be in the store or back in the kitchen working. Nobody would be around, and on some occasions, I'd have the front door locked, so I would be totally alone. But, on those occasions, I'd feel a hand on my back, or my shoulder blades, almost as if someone is trying to excuse themselves as they pass by me, and the 'ghost' is trying to be polite and not bump into me.

"Of course, I'd turn around and think, someone is here, but nobody would be present! It has happened so often, I know it's not my imagination, I can feel the hand on my body.

"One day, we were working in the kitchen preparing the chocolate. The large garbage can lid was just shoved off the top off the container by these unseen hands, and it slid off the top, crashing onto the floor. It landed about six feet away from where it started out! How could that have happened?

"We all just stood there in disbelief, looking at that garbage can lid that is now on the floor, wondering, how in the world, or what could have caused the lid to just fly off and land on the floor! It shook us all up!

"We all just stopped what we were doing. Nobody wanted to go over and pick it up or touch it! We just stared at it, maybe waiting for it to rise up again and land on top of the garbage can!

"Soon, the same thing occurred with the lid of the blender! We were working in the kitchen, and those same unseen hands shoved that lid off of the blender and it landed on the floor.

"On another occasion, something caused the antique bourbon decanters out in the showroom to just lay down!

"We'd heard a strange sound, completely different than anything we'd heard ever, so we left the kitchen and we went out to investigate. It sounded like a crash!

"Look up here on this high shelve. That is a collection of antique bottles that we had acquired, just for atmosphere and the bourbon connection with the place. One of them just had landed over. It was placed on the second shelf, and then, it was on its side, on the lower shelf.

"Now, we've got the bottles secure, to prevent any accidents or anything, and we definitely don't want the bottles to fall. They are antiques.

"Something created that strange noise, almost like a crash or a bang sound, and the one bottle was just on its side, as if some hand had reached up and laid it on its side," said Kelly.

I wanted to hear from employee Stacy, to know what she had to say, or what she had experienced.

"Fred is our ghost. He' hasn't scared me as such, but I don't like it when I'm touched by something," began Stacy.

"A while back, someone was here who had some history on the offices down here, and the gentleman said a man had died in this office, and his name was Fred. So, we just started calling him Fred.

"I've seen shadows in the back room, mostly on the other side of the wall that divides the kitchen area and the back," Stacy explained.

"What's back behind the wall, an exit?" I asked.

"No, it's just a storage area, no exit whatsoever. When you are back here, there is only way one in and one way out, and it is out the front door. So that eliminates anyone working back there, or exiting the store without your knowledge," added Stacy.

"One other thing worth mentioning here," Kelly said, "is that our scale in the back room gets all out of whack.

"We have to keep it programed so each piece of candy will have the same amount of bourbon and such, and the numbers on the scale will just go crazy! The numbers will get all out of sequence, and the scale is way too new for crazy stuff like that to happen. Something is messing with the scale!"

"Can you explain it more?" I asked.

"I have to always, recalibrate the scale at the beginning for accuracy. We can place candy in the dish for weighing and notice the weigh in the window. Then, without any rhythm or reason, it will be as if a hand it pressing down, causing the numbers in the display window to increase in weight!

"Then the opposite will sometimes happen! Candy will be in the dish and the weight recording, then it will be as if, something is lifting up the dish and the weight will decrease.

"And it's not just in the one scale, we've got two scales and the same thing happens. I change the batteries thinking that will solve the problem, and it doesn't!" continued Stacy.

"We just blame it on Fred!" both ladies said.

Stacy added, "Objects will be moved around, we'd sit something down in one area, turn around, and minutes later it is gone, and sure enough, it will turn up somewhere else!

"I've felt cool breezes blowing around in there, when no air conditioning would be on. The temperature of the room would just drop and become chilly.

"Maybe it's my imagination, but that is when it seems like stuff starts happening, maybe the cool temperature is like the warning of something that is to come, almost like a forewarning or something.

"I don't think anyone is afraid of Fred, if that is our ghost; and the ladies here, just about accept having him around.

"The guys, on the other hand, including my husband Forest, aren't for sure it is haunted or not. Those guys are always looking for logical explanations. They can look for answers all they want to, but I know what I've felt, experienced, and seen to know better."

"As long as Fred keeps out of the bourbon and our chocolate, he can hang around!" said Kelly.

Fox Hollow Farm doesn't look too haunted from the outside, but with a history of murder, it is haunted, and deeply troubled too.

An Investigation at Fox Hollow, Indianapolis, Indiana.

When the opportunity presents itself to share an investigation with my readers, I do like to seize it and share that experience. Most of this narrative would be considered an excerpt from all the events that occurred that night.

The location for this investigation is at the Fox Hollow Farm, just slightly north of Indianapolis, Indiana, in the community of Carmel.

Fox Hollow was the setting of a gruesome serial killer's lifestyle from the early 1980s. The property also had the association or was rumored to be, a part of the I-70 killer/stranger. Fox Hollow was the home of the infamous killer, Herb Baumeister. After the property setting almost in an abandon state for over a decade, it was sold in 2009, so today, the property is privately owned.

For this passage, I'm going to respect the homeowner's privacy and not reveal his real name. The homeowner and his wife agreed to open up their home for a group of ghost investigators. The mansion is haunted with the ghosts of at least, 11-15 gay men who were murdered there by the hands of Herb Baumeister.

What I'm about to share with you are the details of the investigation that occurred that night.

The homeowner had made arrangements to have to only one of the survivors to be in attendance and to share his memory of that night. For this writing, the one survivor will be identified by this alias as Mark.

About twenty ghost investigators made plans to be there that evening. Once we all assembled in the circular driveway out front, we were greeted by out hostess. She led us inside the stately front doors, and we grouped in the main hallway. It was at this point, where all introductions were made, which was the homeowner, and Mark.

The homeowner shared some paranormal experiences that his wife has saw. He said that his wife has seen a man in the woods, just out of the bathroom window, on the west side of the house. He said that his wife saw a man, wearing a red shirt, yet, he had no legs. Even though she saw no legs, she was able to see his upper torso move about, near the woods of the secluded property. His wife had actually seen this ghostly figure on two prior occasions, before she even mentioned it to him.

He said, that another haunted location takes place in the basement, and he encouraged us to make sure we visit that room. He stated, that while he would be running the vacuum cleaner in the billiards room, something continually unplugged the vacuum cleaner! He said that he finally became frustrated, and cried out, "*Stop unplugging the vacuum, I need to sweep this carpet.*" The spirt or ghost, was agreeable, and stopped unplugging the vacuum cleaner!

An orb, near the corner of the indoor pool room.

While in the basement, another location that is a must to visit would be his locker room. It is a large room, opposite of the billiards room, and across from the indoor pool. This bathroom doubles as a changing room, with the usual bathroom plumbing, plus a row of lockers, and in one end, a sauna. This bathroom also had benches, much like one would see in a school locker room.

Over the years that the homeowners have resided here, different psychics and paranormal groups have toured and investigated the house. This particular bathroom, has been labeled as a portal for spirits to come and go. He then added, that his particular bathroom, is a room where his wife prefers not to use or enter at all. She has reported that the room caused the hair stand up on the back of her neck.

Psychics and experienced ghost investigators reported back to the homeowners, that the souls have not moved on to the next world, simply because so many have not been identified, and no closure has come to their passing. Their souls are without rest. Most of the investigators did conclude that the spirits that remain, aren't demonic, other than Herb.

Of course, the final location in the mansion that will be worth our time to investigate, and linger, is the indoor pool room. According to the crime reports and history associated with the house's violent past, the majority of the killings occurred in the pool and the adjacent rooms (the billiard's room) and with this assumption, the pump room.

The homeowner continued by saying, that a tenant who resided in the upstairs apartment was using the indoor pool. He was swimming alone when something came up from behind him, and grabbed him by the neck. He could feel the strength of the hands on his shoulders and neck, as if in an attempt to push him under the water. Then, the force just stopped. He promptly got out of the swimming pool.

The homeowner and Mark, both told us as an investigative team that the pump room, that is adjacent to the indoor pool, was full of negative energy. It has been reported by others, that a shadow like figure has been seen, moving from right to the left in the pump room. Nobody knows for sure, if any time of sexual assaults or murders occurred in the pump room, but as we were told, other paranormal investigators had experienced sensations in that.

I'm using dowsing rods in the indoor pool room.

I stepped into the room alone, hoping to feel some of the negative energy. I didn't like the room for some reason, maybe because of the darkness and the sounds of the running pool filters and equipment to purify the water, but it wasn't a room that I was comfortable being inside of. I didn't get anything with the usage of my dowsing rods, nor did I have any luck with any pictures on my camera. I didn't linger in the room, any longer than I felt necessary.

My group had gathered in a large locker room, just opposite of the indoor swimming pool. We had been told that on previous investigations and times of research, that this particular room had a lot of energy. Our guide, Mark had joined us. In the room was not only myself, but my two companions on the trip, Cathy Smith and her sister, Ellen Waddle. Plus, one other woman, whom I didn't know, happened to be in the room with us.

Mark was trying to communicate with Herb's alter ego, Brian Smart. Mark was doing all the speaking to Brian Smart. Ellen Waddle, who happened to be new to an investigation, was learning to use my dowsing rods. Mark, the three women, and I were standing almost in a circle, all facing one another.

"Brian, Brian, this is Mark, I know you're here, just let us know by pushing the dowsing rods. Come on Brian, I'm here in peace with friends, who want to have some contact with you," said Mark.

People have spoken of being pushed up and down the stairs of the Fox Hollow Mansion.

We all stood silently, just listening and watching Ellen holding the dowsing rods.

"Come on, Brian, let us know you're here, don't be shy," continued Mark.

No sounds were heard, and the dowsing rods haven't moved. Mark continued to invite the ghost of Brian Smart to do something.

"Brian, if you're here with us, push open the rods, come on, you can do it."

The four of us stood silently, watching and waiting, until the rods slowly opened.

Ellen's eyes opened widely, and she whispered to us, "It's not me, I can feel the rods being pushed open!"

Mark praised Brian for his movement with the rods. Mark continued to ask Brian to make his presence known.

"Brian, let's think about what all happened here, come back into the house, and into this very room. Think about the woods, the woods that are behind this very house, the woods that you know, very well.

"Brian, I know you can do this, I want you to push the dowsing rods, and push the rods and point to the person here, that you'd like to take out back, and into the woods.

"Come on, Brian, show me, who you'd like to take into the woods.

The rods slowly turned, to face the woman who was standing to my right, whom none of us knew.

"Good, Brian, you pushed the rods to this lady right here. Is there anyone else? Go on, Brian, push the rods to the person you'd like to take to the woods."

The rods slowly turned, and the two rods at this time, pointed to me. My breathing became heavy, and almost like a cold sensation came over my body.

Ellen and I fixed our eyes upon each other, with the rods pointing toward me.

"I'm not doing this with the rods," said Ellen, as if I had doubts. "They are moving on their own."

"Come on Brian, is there anyone else here, that you'd like to take to the woods?

By now, several people had gathered into the doorway of this bathroom and were watching this period of communication. The rods moved to Cathy Smith. There was some gasping and whispering now coming from the spectators in the hallway. We all pretty much had the same thought, and that is, one person is left here. Is Brian finished or will the rods point to Mark?

"Brian, is there anyone else here, in this room, that you'd like to take to the woods?"

We knew what was going to happen. The rods moved to Mark and stopped, pointing at him.

"Brian, you want all four of these people to go with you to the woods, right? If that is so, spread open the rods to show us either a yes or no response," said Mark.

As Ellen held the rods, the two dowsing rods parted and moved into the yes position. We all knew what that meant, the ghost of Brian Smart, whom Mark had been communicating with, wanted the four of us to go with him on a walk in the woods.

We all looked at one another, exchanging the glances and waiting for the nods of approval. None of us spoke but silently exited the bathroom, into the hallway, into the billiards room, and outdoors. Mark was the leader, and the only sounds heard were our own footsteps traipsing through the cold leaves and brush on the ground. Mark led us to a clearing, not too far from the house. We could see the windows that were lit, and a few outdoor lanterns.

The door knocker knocks on its own, and nobody is on the other side wanting indoors.

"This is the area, where if you'll notice, nothing grows. Look upwards, and you'll see only the five trees, with the tree limbs overhead, trees that are growing a circle, yet nothing grows on this ground.

"Please follow me, and step in my footsteps. Let's all walk in a clockwise position in a circle, right in this area. Brian, come and join us, we've followed your directions and we're outside in your area."

After about two or three rotations of all of us walking in the circle, and within the single file line, Mark begin to trail off, down a ravine. It was steep and a path that appeared to be well traveled. We passed trees, and low sprouting limbs, that would slap an unsuspecting walker in the face. The sounds and illumination of the mansion soon fell silent and from sight, and only the light of the moon was our guiding light.

Mark had us to stop, and group around him.

Blessings upon the house and guardian angels.

"This is an area where one of the bodies was found, and you'll see, nothing grows in this haunted soil.

Journeying on, we came to another area and stopped.

"Another body was found here. Bloody, lifeless, buried in a shallow grave, that was unearth by the Indiana FBI.

"Brian, we're here, we're outside, speak to us through the rods.".

Nothing but silence. The rods didn't move, but we stared at one another, just waiting for something to happen.

Mark reached out his hands toward Ellen, and she handled him the rods.

"Brian, push open the rods, to let us know, you're with us. Come on, you can do it," as he spoke with encouraging words.

The rods barely moved to the open position.

We all stood there, staring at the rods, and looking at one another. Nobody said anything. We were all just waiting for whatever direction Mark was going to give to Brian, or if Brian was going to do anything at all.

The energy level is weak at this point, maybe because we're so far from the energy that is in the house. Brian is having a hard time, working the rods.

"Brian, if you're here, push open the rods," said Mark.

"We had stronger energy in the house," I commented. "Unless, the deceased who were buried here, have pulled the energy away from Brian, and he's not able to do anything at this point."

"Whether the energy is strong or weak, we followed Brian's direction of going into the woods," commented Mark.

"He led us here for a reason, but he's not ready to reveal that reason at this time. Maybe he just wanted us, as visitors to the mansion, to be led to this area of graves sites for the men he loved.

"Let's head back to the house," said Mark. We all followed him back to the mansion, the same way, along the same path.

Back at the property, Mark led us back to the area of the five trees where we first started.

"As a way of closure, we'll need to walk in a counterclockwise direction," said Mark. Without saying anything, our group started walking in the reverse direction.

I looked up at the limbs of the bare trees that seemed to loom over us, much like black, boney fingers reaching down, to push us, into the ground where many others have been buried on this property.

One by one, we each parted ways and headed toward the lights coming from the mansion.

My group remained on the property until shortly after midnight. It seems like, anything ghostly that was there, had gone unnoticed at this time. Some of the other investigators that had traveled here from Chicago, and other locations in Illinois, were wrapping up their investigations as well. Some of the investigators had gotten pictures and one party, had a recording of voices or talking. We were able to hear the recording earlier in the night when we all grouped together. I got an orb in the indoor swimming pool room. But, as the night passed, it seemed like we were all coming up empty and had nothing else to share. At least my group and I, all felt satisfied with what we had experienced and learned at the property, so it was a successful night.

Now to conclude this story, you are probably wondering about what happened to Herb Baumeister. Herb was never brought to trial, even though he was the prime suspect in the disappearance and murder of many gay men from the Indianapolis area. Was he guilty of such crimes? Nobody knows for sure, at least, 100% sure. But this we do know, in 1996, police authorities recovered more than 5,000 human bone fragments on the property from 11 confirmed bodies.

My team of investigators for the evening, Cathy Smith, her sister Ellen Waddle, and myself. New experiences for the novice investigators, but they left as believers.

To this day, neighbors in the elite subdivisions, and visitors to the property, still speak of unsettling feelings, unexplainable noises, like the seven knocks on the upstairs, apartment door, and the sightings of some partial, apparitions roaming into the house, and on the grounds.

Maybe, you'll get to be so lucky as well.

Barbara's Gift Shop of Ghosts in Stearns, Kentucky

Barbara has owned and managed the Depot Gift Shop for a number of years. She's lived in the Stearns community for a very long time and is pretty much on top of all the comings and goings-on in the neighborhood, and some of those comings and goings involve ghosts.

Barbara's gift shop is located at the bottom of the hill, right by the train tracks, and she shares the building with the depot. Tourists who ride the train back to the National Park, usually drift into her gift shop to look at and purchase her specialty items.

From the railroad side, pedestrians would see several store fronts with three front doors. She did expand the gift shop a couple years ago, so it does occupy two store fronts. The first door leads to the railroad office and it occupies the office space on the second floor. Barbara's gift shop occupies the first two store fronts.

Barbara gave me the grand tour of her gift shop, leading me into the two stores fronts. Tall ceilings, large windows, and the original hardwood flooring all seemed like time has stood still.

"What do you know about these two rooms, or store fronts?" I asked her.

"I do know that this area once was the funeral parlor. But over the years, I knocked down the wall to create a much larger opening for retail space. From what I understand, this area was also part of the funeral parlor as well," she said.

Barbara led me past some displays, and pointed toward a back-stair case, almost like a loft area, but it was blocked from customer usage. Under the landing of the staircase, stands a Coke machine. She also has her cookbook collection in that area of the first floor as well, in the back corner. The steps are right there in the retail area, but it is closed to customers.

"The upstairs is just used by me and my other workers, and customers don't go upstairs. I keep my stock upstairs," said Barbara.

"One summer, I hired a young teen girl to help out. She was alone in the store one day, and something caught her eye. She first noticed that a man was standing at the top of the landing, looking down! He was staring right at her!

"It really did scare her! And it would scare me, too, to glance up and see a man, wearing dark clothing, definitely from another time period, rounded hat, just standing there looking down. She described him as best that she could, but as she said, she didn't stay in the store very long once she saw him! And I don't blame her.

"Then the next thing, she said, he was gone, just as quickly as he appeared. And he wasn't a store customer who had wandered upstairs by mistake. This man was real, like we are.

"Now, knowing this was the funeral home, we just assumed he was the funeral director, but we had no real evidence, and we're glad, that he hasn't come back.

"But here's the twist. A short while later, this same young girl who worked for me   was up in the museum looking at some of the older pictures that someone had donated to be used there.

"Just out of the blue, she stopped, and pointed to a man in one of the pictures, and she cried out, 'That's him! That's the man that I saw standing up on the landing, looking down!'

"Of course, we all gasped, stopped and looked at the photo that someone had donated to be used in an exhibit. Because of the commotion that was overheard, someone in the group that was nearby, joined us. We passed the picture around, and someone did identify that man in the photograph as being one of the undertakers!

"On a different occasion, another one of my employees was working alone in the shop. She was behind the counter, stooped down, just at the fudge counter.

"The store sells fudge and it is displayed in this glass case. The employee was stooped down, and from her viewpoint, and straight through the glass, she could see that a man was standing there.

"She could see his navy-blue trousers, and belt buckle, and dark boots. She said she just assumed it was one of the railroad men who stopped into the store to get something.

"She said, 'I'll be with you in a second,' and when she stood up, there was no man standing there. She had only seen him from his waist down! She saw only the torso! No way someone could have been standing there, and just disappeared out the door without being seen."

Barbara invited me to join her in the adjacent room. "Now you're not going to believe what I'm going to tell you now!

"Look at this hutch. At one time, we had all kinds of John Wayne collectibles displayed here for sale.

"I placed little Christmas lights on the back of the shelves to make the items look nice. We also had a couple little night lights of John Wayne displayed, and they would also light up.

"Several other little John Wayne figurines were there, and movie poster tins were leaning up again the back of the hutch, as well as little black and white pictures. Everything here on this hutch was all John Wayne merchandise.

"At closing time, we had to go in and unplug the Christmas lights, and even the little night lights had to be switched off. Just to be safe, the extension cords were all plugged into a surge protector, so I'd turn that off as well.

"One morning, I came into the shop and all those little night lights and the Christmas lights were all turned on! I was the last person in the shop and the first one in that morning, and I knew for a fact, I had them all turned off and unplugged the extension cord from the surge protector. How did that happen?

"Now here's another strange thing about this John Wayne collection.

"I came in to work one morning and I was the first one to unlock the store. I walked into this room, and all three shelves of the John Wayne merchandise was sitting on the floor! The merchandise wasn't mixed up, scattered about or had any appearance that it had fallen and was lying in a pile. The John Wayne merchandise was in the same arrangement as it had been displayed on the shelves.

"So, picture it like this. All the little figurines were grouped together in the same order as they were on the shelf. The night lights were in the same arrangement, the movie poster tins were all laying on the floor, in the same order that I had them propped up against the back wall of the hutch shelves. Everything was in like a mirror order, just sitting on the floor!

"A few months had passed, and I'd moved away all the John Wayne merchandise and I now, set up a collection of little glass objects, vases, and some antique looking clocks. The hutch was filled with new merchandise of collectibles.

"I had a decorative clock that was meant to hang on the wall displayed. It was a small clock with a little hook ring at the top. I inserted a little S hook screw into the top edge of the first shelf, so the little clock would hang down and it was with a collection of merchandise on the second shelf.

"I had an employee in here, and I was telling her all the hauntings that were associated with this hutch. I had told her all about the John Wayne merchandise and how it was left on the floor. She looked at me in disbelief, and said jokingly, 'Okay ghost, do something to prove it to me.'

"We both just stood there, as if waiting for something exciting to happen, but nothing did. We just looked at each other, giggled a little, and walked into the other showroom and began setting out merchandise.

"We heard this crash sound, like a bang, of something heavy falling down and hitting the floor hard.

"We rushed into the room to see what the ruckus was all about. To our astonishment, we both stood there, just staring down at the floor.

"Right in front of the hutch, balanced perfectly was the clock. Now, the clock wasn't sitting on the flat bottom frame, but it was balanced on its edge.

"I looked up at the hutch, and the S hook was still in place. Now, explain to me how that S hook screw was still in place, and how the clock would have been lifted upward and landed, perfectly balanced on its edge?

"Now come with me, over here, and try to explain this ghostly situation.

"The store was closed, and I had another employee in here with me. The county school board had purchased from me 40 gifts all the same, to be handed out during Teacher Appreciation Week. The other employee and I had set up some long, banquet tables and we had almost an assembly line going. We had the gifts ready, the decorative gift bags, the tissue paper, tags, and we'd just take the gift, drop it in the bag, fluff it up with the tissue paper, tag it, and send it down the line.

"One of us would take the packaged gifts and carry them to the front door of the shop and place them in the large boxes. In the morning, someone from the county school board would be coming by to pick up the boxes with the 40 wrapped gifts to be distributed at school the following day.

"It was almost midnight, and we were still wrapping. Both of us had our arms full of wrapped gifts, and we were over here, by the door, organizing the boxes for pick up. We still had a few more to package up and wrap.

"We heard this sound, crash like, and we rushed back to the other side of the store. We couldn't believe our eyes. Something had taken the two, long banquet tables down, folded up the legs, and leaned them against the bookshelf rack that is full of the cookbooks.

"Keep in mind, the tables didn't collapse, the legs were folded up, and the tables moved and leaned up!

"We didn't have any gifts or gift bags on the table, so there wasn't a mess on the floor.

"We just unfolded the tables and continued wrapping. We wrapped at a pretty fast pace this time around, and we were done and out of there by 1 AM.

"Now out in the depot, Park Rangers reported seeing a man in the lobby of the train station. This would be when the train depot was closed, and all the doors locked. The figure, or ghost of a man, is seen walking around in the building. He was spotted walking toward the area where the Whistle-stop Restaurant is today; however, that area wasn't a restaurant. It was unused space. The Park Ranger followed the man, and before he could actually get close enough to call out or stop the man, he just disappeared into that area. The Park Ranger said that he appeared to be gray in appearance.

"The last thing that I can recall, happened over in one of the neighboring buildings from here, and it is labeled Store #3. One of the teachers from the high school had organized some type of a sleep over and ghost investigation.

"Some investigators from out of town came down to help the youngsters get more out of the experience. They had some equipment in there to demonstrate to the students.

"The investigators had a recording device, and one of the students asked, 'Are you a coal miner?'

"After listening to the recording during a playback, the response came back, 'No.'

"Now that might not seem like a big deal, but for the students to be able to hear a response of 'No' really did excite them quite a bit."

Barbara was a very gracious host to spend her time and tell me all her stories. From my standpoint, it's always exciting when things happen that just can't be explained. Objects get moved, sounds are heard, and even apparitions appear in illogical places. All lead us to believe that a place is haunted, and I'm happy for Barbara and that she is operating not only a gift shop for tourists, but also a haunted location that is rich in history. I'm also excited to hear that the students were able to hear an audible response. That really does firm up the belief that a piece of property is haunted. You never really know what or who could turn up next, or for what reason. They might just appear to make their presence known, and to touch the lives of the living so they won't be forgotten.

The stately museum houses not only antiques and artifacts of McCreary County, but a few ghosts as well.

Ghostly Traces at the Stearns, Kentucky Museum

The only thing missing on this summer morning was thunder and lightning. The skies had provided us with ominous looking clouds and a steady rain. This was kind of the rain that causes the windshield wipers to pound out a rhythm, a rhythm that was keeping in time with whatever was playing on the radio. It was hard to believe this was a summer morning in June, and not a late day in November. We had just crossed from Whitley County into McCreary County, traveling a two-lane highway that had way too many ups and downs of the pavement, and plenty of twists and turns that required both hands to be on the steering wheel.

"Look at that old, white horse, standing in that barn," I said to my cousin Joyce Parker.

"I wonder if the owners named that horse 'ghost' just to be funny." I added.

The reason for this journey was simple. Joyce Parker and I decided to visit one of Kentucky's historical attractions, located in the foothills of the Appalachian Mountains of southeastern Kentucky, in the tiny town of Stearns, Kentucky.

Stearns, Kentucky, is located in McCreary County. It's a small town that was once a bustling coal town center, with smaller coal camps leading away from Steans in various directions. Stearns would have been the headquarters for the men who labored in the dangerous conditions of the coal mines. This area saw a rise and fall of life and generations of births and deaths. For a period of 60 plus years or more, this town of Stearns would have been the center of activity. The area of coal mines slowly died out during the late 1950s, and today, it's just a faded memory of a time gone by. This area is now a tourist attraction for visitors to get a sampling of what this part of Kentucky history would have been like.

Along the few streets that remain, stands that actual building from that time period. The buildings were all painted in the soft lime green color, trimmed in white. The few businesses had creative names for the time, Store #1, and Store #3. We later found out that Store #2 was out in a prosperous coal camp. A few empty lots were there, no doubt, buildings that were lost due to fire or some other calamity for wooden framed buildings of that time period.

From the parking lot, our attention was drawn to this large, imposing structure perched high upon a hill. It appeared to have twenty or more concrete steps to reach the front porch. The white framed building, trimmed in dark green, had two floors with multiple windows scattered across the front. On the third floor, two sets of dormer windows were placed, and each set had triple windows, for a total of six windows.

By the lack of sunshine on this rainy morning, each window provided a perfect vantage point for any individual, living or deceased, to be peering down watching pedestrians on the sidewalk.

"If that place isn't haunted, it should be," I said to Joyce.

The sign out front read, McCreary County Historical Museum, and this museum was a part of our tour for the day with our admission to the train ride, and the national park. We were greeted by two ladies welcoming the visitors and giving a brief overview of the property.

The ladies introduced themselves as Juanita and Virginia.

"This building was the main office for the Stearns Coal Company," began Juanita.

"So, by the size of this building, it wasn't a hotel?" I jumped in to ask.

"No, the hotel was across the street, and it burned down years ago," answered Virginia.

"Nobody ever lived here, the first and second floors were offices, and the third was used for storage and such. It was never used as a home, or hotel, or anything like that.

"Today, we've got displays set up with artifacts that had been donated by the residents of McCreary County. Several rooms are set up with things that would represent what life would have been like at the time of the coal industry.

"We've got

We can only hope that something ghostly traveled with this historic Post Office when it was relocated to the museum.

displays of what the homes would have looked like, the company grocery store, a bank, an actual front end to the Post Office Bell Farm, Kentucky, and a military collection, too.

"Be sure to visit all the rooms, but unfortunately, the upstairs is off limits. You can go anywhere you'd like on this floor," Virginia said.

Joyce and I roamed about the first floor, snapping quick pictures along the way. We found the grocery store to be fascinating with all the products, bottles, and jars. To complete the exhibit, they had a real screen door that had Merita Bread on the door handle.

Around the corner was the actual, front end mail boxes of the Bell Farm, Kentucky office. I positioned myself just right and pulled out my camera to snap a picture of this architectural treasure. As soon as I pushed the shutter for the picture, I saw in the view finder, this white vapor like image, shoot across the camera screen, much like a rocket! It traveled in an arch, but unfortunately, my camera didn't capture it on the digital. But my eyes sure saw that white mist or 'ghost' as plain as day. I called out to Joyce, who was close by, to tell her about what I had just seen. I snapped a second picture, just to see if I could recapture it a second time, but unfortunately, nothing happened.

We visited on around the exhibits, past the military and the police, and the bank's vaults, and we were now, at the entrance where we first met up with the two employees, Virginia and Juanita. Since nobody else was present beside Joyce and the two ladies, and they appeared to be chatting it up with us, I dropped the question.

"Is this place haunted?" I asked the ladies.

Juanita spoke up first, "Why, yes, it is. Why would you ask? Did you see something?"

I mentioned that in my camera, I saw a white mist, that flew across the camera's view finder right in front of the Bell Farm Post Office window. The camera didn't photograph it, but I saw it.

The ladies began telling me different things about hauntings in the building, and they said that I need to speak with the manager, Shane, as well.

"We've heard the sound of an old, timey typewriter coming from the military room, and we've all heard someone walking about upstairs, when it was just us in the building," said Juanita.

"When we had a group of high school students here volunteering, a couple of the girls screamed, when they saw a ball of light, just descend from the staircase, coming down from the second floor."

"We'll close the upstairs door, and next thing we know, that door is open."

I was still intrigued about the upstairs rooms in this building. I kept walking over there, and looking up the staircase, as if I was expecting to see something.

"Is there any way we could see the upstairs and look around?" I asked the ladies.

The ladies looked at each other, and agreed for a real quick tour, and thought it wouldn't hurt. Virginia led the way.

Is a ghostly spirit inhabiting this bedroom display in the museum? What sprits might have come with this antique furniture?

Joyce, Virginia, and I went upstairs. It has a long hallway down the center, with several rooms on each side.

"Several of these rooms are just used for storage, and nothing else. One day, we'll have these rooms opened for tours," Virginia told us.

"We've got this room set up like a bedroom, and for some reason, nobody likes to go inside this room. Employees will talk about how chilly this room can become, or sounds coming, as if someone is walking about.

"Sometimes the children will play up here in this end room. Some of the kids will talk about hearing children playing in here, moving about, making noises, or our children, will talk about their things being disturbed, or all messed up.

"Employees who are downstairs, talk about hearing footsteps, as if someone is walking around up here, and we know, nobody is up here."

I snapped a quick picture as we headed down the hallway. I was able to get two orbs in my photo. I showed them to Joyce and Virginia, and Virginia just nodded in agreement as if that's confirmation of some paranormal experiences here.

Two orbs were captured in this photograph on the second floor of the museum. This area is off limits to the public.

We did look around in a couple other rooms, but our guide had nothing to add about the paranormal events or any activities.

Once back downstairs in the lobby, we were able to meet the museum manager, Shane Gilcrest.

"Here comes Shane, and you can ask him about ghosts," said Virginia.

Shane had heard some of our conversation, so he joined right in. "I was in my office just a few minutes ago, and someone came along and opened and then closed my office door. I stopped, walked over and opened the door. I looked around and saw nobody in the hallway, and so I returned to my office and went about my work. Then I heard the door knob rattle, as if someone was turning the knob. I walked over to open the door, and since it is a frosted glass, I should have seen someone on the other side, but nobody was there! I opened the door.

"I did look around in the hallway, and just thought no more of it since I didn't see anyone."

Shane, the ladies, my cousin Joyce, and I just exchanged glances, thinking over what we'd just heard, and experienced upstairs. From my observations, the place is haunted, but it is debatable as to whether the staff of the museum will agree with me 100%.

Shane encouraged me to find a former employee named Dawn. Dawn and Shane had had some conversations about ghosts on a previous occasion, so he thought she would be another great resource.

I was able to locate Dawn at one of the tourist gift shops down by the depot.

Dawn worked as a volunteer in the museum a number of years ago, and she is pretty much the lead historian for the genealogy department of McCreary County.

"I was working the museum, and on more than one occasion, I'd hear footsteps moving about upstairs. I'd heard the footsteps before, and I'd heard the ghost stories from the other folks around here about this place being haunted," said Dawn.

"I wasn't going to just run and jump on the haunted bandwagon without some proof. I wanted some evidence or something.

"Then one day I was alone and working in the museum, and I got tired of hearing all the footsteps, and all the commotion going on upstairs.

"I can only describe it by the sound of a heavy work boot, a step, and then, it would like the next step, and heavy sound on the wooden floor. Then, it would happen again, the same gait of someone slowly walking, and not walking in a normal gait of someone walking. Someone being sneaky, suspicious type of movement.

"I'd go upstairs and look around and see nothing and the strange noises would stop for a bit.

"Finally, after hearing various noises and such, I just called out, 'If you're a ghost, prove it! Do something, or just stop making all these footstep noises and stop that commotion!'

"As soon as I said that, everything stopped! No noises, no more footsteps, nothing was heard, so I guess that ghost thought that I meant business," exclaimed Dawn.

It's uncertain what is haunting the museum, or who it is, and why. But the employees are in agreement that something is still lingering in the museum. For the most part, whatever is haunting the building, seems to be fairly harmless. The ghosts like to make their presence known and doesn't mind being with the employees. Maybe it is because on a deeper level, the employees who are working there, are doing just that, working to preserve the artifacts, exhibits, and the displays for the visitors who want to learn about what life was like in the Stearns community, many decades ago. It's definitely worth the visit for yourself.

In the Name of the Father, the Son, and the Guardian Ghost of St. John's Catholic Church

The year was 1860. President Lincoln was in the White House when St. John's Catholic Church was consecrated as a house of worship. Fr. Bax was the pastor until the year of 1908.

Eight-year-old Alma Kellner when to church to pray on that fateful December 8, 1909, morning at St. John's Catholic Church. Unfortunately, her prayers went unanswered. Her screams were unheard, and her tears shed just dried on the carpet. Alma Kellner met death, head on in a most sinister way.

Such an unlikely location for a dark, murderous deed.

Fingers immediately were pointed to the custodian, a native of France, a new hire just a month before, by the name of Joseph Wendling. Wendling was the main suspect early on. Wendling had keys to the property, and who was the only suspect who intimately knew the building and the layout of the property, room by room, and board by board.

According to Wendling's wife, it was reported to police during questioning about his untimely departure on or around January 14. Her husband withdrew $100 from their bank account. The police had been led to believe that he was in New Orleans.

Mrs. Wendling professed her innocence and having no knowledge of this little girl's disappearance, even though, after a thorough search of the couple's home, two items of interested were discovered in a trunk that were believed to have belonged to the murder girl. It was discovered in the house, that a ring and a pin, that had been positively identified as being property of the deceased child, were given to her by a boy.

Still, after an investigation and search of the Wendling residence, more circumstantial evidence was found that linked Mr. Wendling to his unspeakable crime. Clothing worn by Mr. Wendling was found with blood stains. A hat was recovered from an old barrel, and it too, showed blood stains.

Six months had passed. Alma's dismembered body was discovered in the cellar of the church. A nationwide manhunt began. Mr. Wendling was apprehended in San Francisco, California. He was returned to Louisville, Kentucky, where he was tried, convicted and sentenced to life imprisonment for Alma's murder. He was paroled nearly 24 years later, and he returned to France.

The police pieced this scenario together as they detailed the events of that day.

Alma was a third-grade student at St. Mary's Academy, on East Broadway. Her teachers and the Sisters considered her to be 'adventuresome, bright, and full of promise.' According to Sister Mary Genevieve, "Alma would often steal away from the other children and go to the chapel to spend a moment in prayer. Her devotion to the Child Jesus was amazing."

The report stated that on the morning of December 8, 1909, Alma disappeared. She was last seen on her way to attend morning mass at St. John's Catholic Church, on the corner of Walnut and Clay streets. The church wasn't far from her home.

It was first thought that Alma had been kidnapped and she was being held for ransom. However, the theory was discounted. No ransom demands were ever made.

Her parents, Frederick and Florence Kellner, the granddaughter of John F. Kellner, and the niece of Frank Fehr, wealthy brewers in Louisville, were all grieved and heartbroken. The police were baffled as to what could have happened to the precocious child.

The police felt certain that Mr. Wendling murdered the child as she knelt in prayer. The theory was that he kidnapped the child from the alter and dragged her body into a small, trap door concealed into the floor. From indication, there was an attempt to burn her body in the church furnace, but that attempt had failed. Items found near Alma's body included a gauntlet glove, her handkerchief, and two men's handkerchiefs all covered in blood.

But this story doesn't end here nor does the ghost story begin.

Another character to this story, who came into the church with a sullied past, was Fr. Hans B. Schmidt. He was rumored to have been nicknamed, The Killer Priest.

Fr. Schmidt was a visiting priest at the church. He was active in the parish from August 1909, until March 1910.

Fr. Schmidt was a Roman Catholic priest, and the only one to receive the death penalty in the United States.

Schmidt was born in Germany and ordained there at the Seminary of Mainz in 1904. Schmidt was sent to the United States in 1908, and he was first assigned to St. John's in Louisville, Kentucky. However, turmoil ensued, and Schmidt left St. John's and was transferred to St. Boniface Church in New York City.

While serving at the pastor of St. Boniface, Schmidt got entangled in a love twist with his housekeeper for the rectory, Anna Aumuller. One thing led to another, and Schmidt and Anna were married secretly, and the ceremony was performed by Schmidt himself.

Fr. Schmidt's time with Anna was troubled from the first "I do," even to the point that in the year of 1913, when Hans found out the Anna was pregnant, he slashed her throat on the night of September 2, 1913. He dismembered her body and threw her body's pieces into the Hudson River.

Once the body was discovered, a police investigation led to Fr. Schmidt and he was arrested and charged with the murder. Fr. Schmidt tried to plead insanity which led to a hung jury. In the second trial, he wasn't as fortunate. He was convicted of first-degree murder and sentenced to death in the electric chair. On February 18, 1916, Fr. Hans Schmidt was executed at Sing Sing Prison.

Word made it back to the St. John's parish in Louisville, Kentucky. All of these trial proceeding's had people talking, and wondering, and asking questions.

Was the wrong man convicted of Alma's murder? Was the wrong man, Joseph Wendling wrongfully imprisoned for a murder he didn't commit? Was the real murderer, Fr. Schmidt?

Time moved on for the congregation of St. John's. Time wasn't kind to the parish either. With the decline of the Louisville neighborhood, St. John's Catholic Church closed its doors and ceased to be known as a house of worship. It still bears the name of St. John's, but today, it is the St. John's Men's Shelter. The property and building today, serves men who need a place to stay for the day, receive counseling, assistance with housing, job placement, or just some medical treatment for minor issues. It's staffed by volunteers and paid employees.

On my initial visit to St. John's Men's Shelter, I met a counselor by the name of Mr. Gordon.

I didn't know what to expect once I walked into the building. Some traces of the Catholic Church remain, which I'm grateful for. Even though the building has been repurposed, I can still see it as a house worship. The stained-glass windows are still there, and painted scriptures remain on the walls.

Mr. Gordon, a young man in his early thirties introduced himself. Just his appearance in a maroon sweater, beige jeans, and high-top sneakers he put me at ease immediately. His eyes lit up talking about the building, its mission, and ghosts. He was eager to share with me his experiences. "Yes, I do believe the building is haunted from the ghost of the little girl, Alma, who was killed here."

"What makes you believe the building is haunted? Have you seen or felt anything?" I asked.

"I open up the building in the morning, so I'm the first person here to unlock doors and turn on the lights. Knowing I'm alone in the building, sometimes, I just see an image off to the side, or a shadow, or possibly a sound is heard. Sometimes, I hear sounds of footsteps following me, and I know they aren't mine.

Pointing downward, he said, "My sneakers don't make any type of a sound when I walk across this tiled floor. I just call out, 'Good morning, Alma' and go on my way. Most of the time, the sounds all stop.

"But I feel as if someone is here, in the building with me.

"With the nature of this shelter, and the clients that walk through the doors, sometimes, the unfortunate happens here," he said.

"What do you mean, the unfortunate happens?" I asked.

He walked near to some white tables that were set up, and a couple men were seated at the tables, just staring into space, in silence. I followed him. He pulled out a chair, and I did likewise, and we both sat down.

"Men can come into the shelter and spend the day, no questions asked. That's why the doors are open. On two different occasions, when we'd go to close up, and sometimes we have to ask the men, to leave for the day. Two men, during the course of the day, had sat in their chairs, made no contact with anyone, and just died. That's most unsettling, to realize that clients had passed just sitting here.

"We had one other client to have died in the shower room.

"Unfortunately, not everyone who walks in here, has a happy ending, but that's why we are here," he said.

I thanked Mr. Gordon for his time, and insight into the building's ghost.

On a second visit to the shelter, I was able to meet up with one of the directors, another counselor, and the maintenance man. All three were happy to talk with me about Alma, her history in the building, and possibly, her ghostly spirit.

Ms. Marion Price is one of the directors of the shelter. She greeted me in her office and was quick to show me a picture.

The picture she showed me was taken during a recent renovation and remodeling of the building. The photographer wasn't trying to get anything ghostly or supernatural. The photographer was in the balcony and was actually documenting the progress of the restoration of the ceiling. Scaffolding was up and painters had been working on the ceiling.

The picture, a 5 x 7, was framed and on Marion's desk. She handed it to me.

I gasped as I looked at the photo. "Hundreds of orbs are in the photograph. They are of all sizes, and some appear to be in a darker white color, while some smaller ones appear to be more translucent," I commented as I handed the picture back to her.

Marion showed me a couple other pictures that were taken by the same photographer within seconds, almost like pictures in a series. Those pictures had no orbs in them whatsoever.

Marion and I walked out into what was once the sanctuary of the church. Marion pointed up to a large statue of Mary.

"I do feel like something is here, and whether it is Alma or something else, remains to be known. However, I don't always refer to Alma as a ghost, I refer to her as my 'guardian angel, or guardian ghost' if you will.

Is Alma the shelter's guardian ghost?

"Strange and almost dangerous things have occurred in this building, and when they happen without any harm or serious damage, I give the credit to Alma, for being our guardian ghost," Marion said

"Look at the statue of Mary in the niche on the left. Look at the statue of Joseph, in the niche on the left. Notice all the molding that is around the statue on the left. That's massive carving, and it's probably been attached to the wall, surrounding the statue since the building of the church.

"One morning for no reason, the molding that encircled the statue of Mary just came crashing down! A large crash was heard and the wooden molding, didn't just collapse and fall straight down, but it fell outward.

"It crashed through the drop-down ceiling that we'd installed years ago into this men's room. It's our shower room today, with the other plumbing on the other side of the room.

"Here's the miracle. On that particular day we had a charity group to come down and serve lunch. We're don't normally serve food here, so this was a rare occasion. All the men were out here waiting to be served. Had this been any other day, we would have had men in that restroom area and most likely, had men in the shower room.

"That molding falling at that height and crashing through the ceiling like that, would have killed the men in the showers.

"And like I said, it didn't just fall straight

Prayers are offered up daily for the living and the deceased, who have passed through the doors.

down, it almost jumped away from the wall and landed hard on the floor. Nothing else was disturbed at all. We all heard the loud crash sound, and we went running!

"I can't help but think that Alma was responsible as a guardian ghost angel. There was nobody hurt. In fact, nobody was in the area at all, thanks to the good people who had brought down a lunch for our clients.

"We've also had times of financial hardship, almost to the point of having to close our doors. We've explored every avenue for financial assistance and leave here befuddled at the end of the day, wondering how we'd meet our expenses.

"At times, when I'm in here alone, I can't help but think about Alma and how dedicated she was to the church that she loved so much. If she can still hang around here, so can we.

"Out of the blue, we'd receive a donation, or a grant, or some monetary gift that answered our prayers and help us to keep our doors open.

"I'd say that deep down, even though Alma had such a tragic ending to her life, she's still here and wants our work here to continue," said Marion.

On my particular visit, besides Marion, I was with a counselor named Keith, and a maintenance worker, Charles.

Neither of the two men denied or confirmed the existence of ghosts or Alma's spirt in the building, but both are open to the possibility. Both agreed that something could be in the building serving as a guardian angel.

Charles led us, including Marion and Keith, outside of the building to the rear of the structure. There are the cellar doors. We went into the basement to look around.

"I'm down here quite a bit," began Charles. It does have the original brickwork and flooring, and an area, just under the sanctuary, where possibly, her body could have been buried.

We walked over and stood next to a brick foundation, that on the other side, had been filled with dirt. The foundation wall came up to about 4.5 feet high. HVAC work and operations were nearby, with duct work scattered throughout.

"If anything is down here, it's keeping its peace with me," Charles continued.

We all walked around and studied the ceiling. According to one crime report, it was said that Alma's body was lowered down thought a trap down in the floor. We searched but found no evidence. The floor joists all appeared to be original, worn, and chalky gray in appearance.

We exited the basement and returned back to the rear of the building. The exterior door led us into the back of the church, in an adjacent room to the sanctuary.

Keith and I continued our tour of the building. We had reached the back of the sanctuary, by the doors that would lead out onto Muhammad Ali Blvd. A receptionist desk is in the center, near the doorway, just under the balcony. Two offices for counselors are in the back of the building. Other partitions have been places on both the east and west walls to create additional office space.

I was interested in visiting the bell tower. We entered a small room that was being used as storage. Keith showed me to the location and opened the wooden door that led to the bell tower.

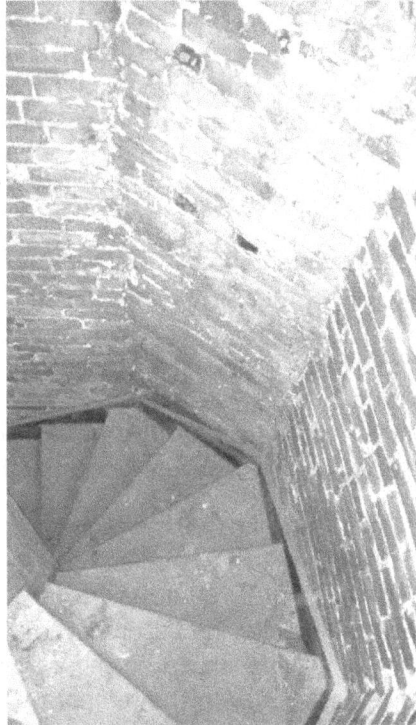

Could a ghostly spirit be trapped in this spiral staircase?

Inside, weather worn, wooden spiral steps led upward. The bell tower was dimly lit with only natural light from outside, but I ascended to the top, or as far as I could safely go. One pointed window opening allowed in natural light. Cobwebs cascaded the sides and grit was on the steps. I could see my own footprints on the steps and my finger prints broke the covering of dust on the rough, brick walls. I could only go so far upwards, unfortunately, not to the tower. It had been boarded and closed off, probably when the bells were removed. I touched and pushed on the wooden covering, but it wouldn't budge.

Descending the wooded steps was easier than the climb up. Since it was all spiral, I'd reached the bottom before I realized it and continued to turn. I'd not noticed the exit door that would have led me back into the storage room. The staircase suddenly came to an abrupt ending. I had gone a couple steps past the main floor and came face to face with a wall.

The wainscoting wall paneling had been placed over the steps.

"Keith," I called out, "This wall doesn't look right." He joined me in the narrow location. "This isn't an original wall and looks strange. This looks like it could be an opening!" I said to Keith.

"As many times I've been in this room and looking into the tower, I've never stepped in this spot, nor paid any attention to this wall," Keith answered me.

Keith and I poked around at the wall. We had no trouble at removing the paneling. Behind the paneling was the rest of the staircase going into the basement.

It wasn't hard for us to piece this together. Here's the so-called trap door that was referenced by the police report.

Is this the passageway, that over 100 years ago, either Fr. Schmidt or the custodian, Mr. Wendling was responsible for dragging Alma's body to the basement? Is this the same staircase that he descended into the basement to dispose of her body?

It appears to be the passageway not only to the basement, but the passageway to the temporary burial grounds for Alma.

We both stood there in silence, looking at the opening of the staircase. Keith closed the door, and gave it a good shove, making sure it remained closed.

Maria had joined us to see what we'd discovered. We shared with her our finding. She also had no idea that panel was at the location in the bell tower. Nothing else needed to be said at that point, our silence, and our stare at the now closed panel said enough.

One by one we left that area, and moved back into the storage room, and Keith closed the door that led into the bell tower room.

"I've got something else of interest to show you, if you'll come this way into this room. I've got some security video that was recently recorded," she said.

The three of us gathered around this one computer, and Maria was able to show us some strange phenomenal. On one particular night, the motion detector with the video camera, picked up an image in the main sanctuary. The motion detector picked up movement, an image that was gliding, or almost floating across the sanctuary.

Maria was able to find another video that was activated when it picked up more ghostly activity in the building.

I asked about the cameras and their location, and Maria pointed them out in the sanctuary. Something was definitely moving about, the white image appeared, would move, and then, fade away.

"Whatever it is, sure has been active," I commented to Maria.

"I'd like to invite you to an event that we hold every December 21st. This is a solemn occasion that we as the staff put together. Everyone is welcome, and we invite any clients, family members, supporters, to come down here. On that December day, or the first day of winter, we always dim the lights and light candles, here the building that was once, a holy place of worship. Different ones on staff call out the names of those men, or women, who were served here, and had died that past year. Family members can speak on behalf of their deceased loved ones.

"It's our way of remembering those folks, who hold a place in our hearts and our memories and need to be remembered in some way and not be some forgotten souls.

"We hold one name till the last, to make sure each person's name is called first. Then, Alma's name is always recited, and we pause long enough to remember that little girl's life that was so tragically cut short by the hands of a crazed killer. She's held in regard as one of our guardian ghost angels who is watching over us.

"Our service concludes with the singing of *Silent Night*, with every voice singing by the glow of the candlelight, allowing each voice to echo in unison through the building.

"I'm sure Alma hears this," said Marion.

"And with the song lyrics, it's longer a 'silent night, or a lonely night for Alma," I said.

"May she rest in peace," Maria commented.

Investigation at the Culbertson Mansion
New Albany, Indiana

The Culbertson Mansion of New Albany, Indiana retains is architectural glory and its ghosts.

In August of 2018, the curator and management of the historic home that once belonged to the millionaire William Culbertson, organized its first ghost investigation. The event was open to the public and I was thrilled to be a part of this ghost investigation.

At least 30 guests, some of whom had no ghost investigating experience, as well as knowledgeable investigators were in attendance. Excitement filled the air with some sharing previous encounters at the house as novice investigators listened with the hopes of having something spectacular happen to them as well.

In my third book, *Haunted Louisville 3, You Are Never Alone,* I tell of my experiences doing investigations in the house, and some experiences where I wasn't necessarily doing an investigation; I just happened to be in the right place at the right time. This was my first time with a structured investigation led by Joni Mayhan, of New Harmony, Indiana, and her team.

The group met in the parlor of the home for a brief overview of the Culbertson family. It is important to know the history of the property and the names and relationship of the ghosts who have chosen to remain.

As with any family, the Culbertsons were acquainted with joys and sorrows, family strife, the heartbreak of death, remarriage, and countless other events that all have left imprints on the property.

Over the years, the house changed hands multiple times, and thank goodness, didn't fall to the wrecking ball. In the 1960s, a gas station was slated to be on that corner of the property.

This is pure speculation, but we have no real knowledge that the ghosts who do linger inside this 25-room mansion are all Culbertson family members. Some of the ghosts could be servants of the Culbertsons. A few of the ghosts could be from previous owners or even, when the property was used by a social club non-profit. But no matter what ghosts are there, they have chosen a remarkable landmark to remain and interact with those of the living, if they so desire.

The leadership of the investigation had the group divided into smaller parties of roughly ten guests each. My group remained in the parlor while the other two groups went elsewhere in the house.

The team from New Harmony, Indiana's paranormal group, had brought some equipment. Instructions were provided on how to make the best use of the tools in the tool bag.

We had a spirit box, dowsing rods, and an EVP meter to use, as well as our own instincts. In our circle, we were able to ask questions using the dowsing rods, just simple questions that would be answered with a yes or no response. Several members in my circle asked questions, such as, 'Is there a ghost present in the room?' 'Are you a member of the Culberson family? And Did you enjoy your life here in this house?"

Some of the responses were in the yes position and some were in the no position.

We had the spirit box placed in the center of the circle. The spirit box scans radio frequencies in the area, so we heard a lot of static, but on occasion, when someone would directly ask a question to the spirit box, the answer would be a reasonable response. Most of the answers were one-word answers. Sometimes the responses would be coming from a male voice, and other times a female voice.

Even with the use of the dowsing rods and the spirit box, we had no guarantee that the parties responding were members of the Culbertson family, house servants, or other entities lingering inside the mansion.

One instance, a guest asked if the spirit was male or female, and after a few seconds, the response came back as female. A second question was asked, trying to gather a little more data on the identity of this female. The reply was of the woman in the portrait on the wall. We sat in silence, looking about the large parlor. Only one portrait hung on the wall of a female. The museum curator was with us at the time, and she responded that the portrait of the female was only a period piece on loan from the Indiana Department of Archives, and the woman in the portrait had no connection to the Culbertson family at all.

Did we contact the woman in the portrait? Nobody knows for sure, but it's strange that the voice from the spirt box, would refer to a woman's portrait hanging in the parlor.

Each group had about 45 minutes in the rooms. My group was to move to the third floor to an upstairs bedroom.

We had a leader from the New Harmony, Indiana paranormal group who was assisting within this room. This was an upstairs bedroom, and the curator of the museum feels like that might have been a bedroom for a house servant or possibility of nanny to the children. The bedroom furniture is not original to the house. It is a collection of period pieces on loan for display in the house.

A second door is on the west side of the room. Through the door is a hallway, which would have led down to the second and first floors, and the kitchen. In the corner of the hallway is what the Culbertson had built to be used at the punishment closet.

The facilitator told us that several of the guests on the investigation tonight had gotten responses from using the dowsing rods in the punishment closet. Since the punishment closet is small, we could only access it by going in pairs of two guests at a time.

Another guest and I went to the punishment closet early in this part of the investigation. The punishment closet is small, with crisscrossed wooden slats that allowed for plenty of air ventilation and light. A chair would have been in the room, but on this night, no chair was in the closet.

I went inside first and closed the door behind me. The air was heavy in there, and most uncomfortable. A feeling of dread washed over me.

Each guest had about three minutes in the punishment closet. I had the dowsing rods in my hands, and I did my best to steady them, but the rods seemed to have a mind of their own. No matter the question that I asked, the rods would continually swing and move as if a force was pushing them. I even braced myself against the wall to help steady the rods. Sometimes, the rods would swing in tandem, other times they would just swing left and right, and cross. I soon realized that what ghosts were in here, didn't want to be bothered or to communicate with me in any form or fashion. My only hope was that the other guests might have better luck. I left the punishment closet with nothing to report.

My situation did change once I joined the others who were still, seated in the circle. I'd returned just in time to hear another woman in our group, exclaim pretty loudly, that something had touched her on the back. Several guests pushed back their chairs to stand up and look for themselves. Nothing was to be seen in the corner.

"I felt something, too, but just thought it was my imagination; but something touched my shoulder," stated another woman, who was seated next to the first woman.

"The temperature in this area of the bedroom is much colder now," said another and he stood up, and walked to the corner of the room.

Nobody said anything for a minute or two. I gingerly moved across the room and took my seat. The room remained quiet.

"There it goes again, the sound of someone walking across the floor!" said another guest. We all turned our heads about and looked in the direction that the sound came from, which was opposite of the location where the two women claimed they had been touched.

The leader of the group asked everyone to just remain quiet and to take their seats. This way, if anything else starts to happen, we should be quiet and still and be ready to see and document the activity. Two or three more minutes passed as we sat quietly. Nothing happened. The two guests who had excused themselves to go work the punishment closet had now returned our group. Two more people left at this time for the punishment closet.

It was my turn to ask questions of the spirit box. I stared at the apparatus in the floor that's still pretty mysterious to me. I wondered what kind of responses I'd get back.

"Did you work as a servant girl in the house?" I asked.

Static was heard coming from the spirit box, and then silence broke the static.

"Yes," came through. We all looked at one another in the room, some had their mouths open in disbelief.

"Ask something else to the servant girl," said the facilitator.

"What was your favorite thing to do in the house?" was my next question.

A few seconds passed, and a minute or two followed with only static coming from the spirit box.

"Eat," was heard in a female's voice that came from the spirit box.

The others looked at me like I had some connection with the servant girl. "Ask something else," said one of the other participants.

I leaned in closer to the spirit box, almost sitting on the each of my metal folding chair.

"What was your least favorite thing to do in the house?" I asked next.

This response came more quickly, without much hesitation.

"Windows," was the female voice.

Laughter broke the silence and the tension eased.

"Windows," said one of the guests, "Did you hear that? Windows."

"We've got something in common with this ghost," I commented to the folks seated next to me. "Nobody wants to wash windows."

"Go on, ask another question," demanded another guest, but before I could go further into the communication realm with this ghost, the other two guests returned from spending time in the punishment closet.

"We could hear laughter all the way down the hallway. What was so funny?" was asked by one of the guests who was in the punishment closet.

The facilitator pointed to me and relayed the situation that I had experienced with the servant girl with the assistance of the spirit box. The laugher came from that she doesn't like to wash windows, and her favorite part of the house was eating.

A knock was sounded on the door and another one of the house volunteers came in to tell us it was time to join everyone in the parlor.

Downstairs, the entire group assembled together, and Joni lead the discussion.

She asked several people if they wanted to share any experiences or to elaborate on what they might have learned for this time in the mansion.

Several mentioned touches on the shoulders and neck, tingling, hair being pulled, or even a chair being pushed across the room.

Different folks commented that they enjoyed their sessions with the dowsing rods. Other chimed in about using the spirit box and the sensation of knowing they are communicating with some spirit.

I couldn't help but wonder if I was the only one able to communicate with a servant girl and she made everyone in our group laugh.

Even though the servant girl is trapped in time, apparently, she and the living have plenty in common. We all like to eat and nobody likes to wash windows.

Knock, Knock, and Nobody's There

Orange Beach, Alabama

I contacted my friend, James Smith about renting his beach front condo for a few days in April of 2017. Unfortunately, James' response wasn't what I wanted to hear; it wasn't available due to another renter.

"Let me give you my neighbor's phone number, she's next door to my condo, and maybe it is available," said James.

I contacted Betty Robinson of Birmingham, Alabama, and her condo was available. I was excited to find beach front lodging on such short notice. I never asked her about the layout or any particulars of her condo, I was just happy it was available and at a rental price that I was willing to pay.

I traveled with a colleague of mine from work, Cathy Smith, and together we made the road trip from Louisville, Kentucky to Orange Beach, Alabama. Betty's condo was just about perfect to meet our needs for these few days at the beach. It was on the third floor of the building, with a loft bedroom upstairs, two baths, kitchen, laundry room, and a living room that had a balcony that overlooked the Gulf of Mexico. The living room also had a sleeper sofa, which I agreed to take. I told Cathy she could have the upstairs loft area to herself. I knew I'd be happy laying on the bed, looking out the glass doors enjoying a view of the Gulf and watching the waves pound the shore.

Nightfall had settled over Orange Beach, and the sound of the waves could be heard in the distance through the open glass doors. Cathy was upstairs getting settled into the loft bedroom. I was in the living room, getting settled.

"Knock, knock! Four distinct knocks came from the door which interrupted my silence. I turned and faced the door to the condo, wondering who might be on the other side. "That's odd, I thought, who would be knocking on the door?"

I walked to the door, opened it, looked all around, and nobody was in sight. I closed the door and checked the lock. Since it was near bed time, I began walking about, turning out the remaining lights, the bathroom, the kitchen, and finally, the two lamps that were on opposite ends of the couch, which was now unfolded, making my bed for the night on the sleeper sofa. The room was dark, and I hadn't fallen asleep yet.

"Knock, knock! Again, four distinct knocks, but this time, the knocking sounds weren't coming from the doorway, but the knocks sounded as if they were only a few feet from where I was laying, coming from the kitchen counter side. The four knocks sounded the very same way that the previous knocks had sounded, with the same amount of force, or strength.

I didn't rise from my bed to walk to the door. I disregarded the knocks originating from the door. The sound of the knocks was way too close. I just laid in the bed, and the first thought that crossed my mind way, *I wonder if this place has a ghost?*

I don't just jump and assume a place is haunted because I hear some strange sounds. I've been in the ghost investigation and storytelling business too long. But I still kept thinking, I *wonder if this place has a ghost*.

When morning came, I asked Cathy Smith if she heard any knocks last night, and she said that she didn't. I explained that I heard two sets, of four distinct knocks, and the first set sounded so real, I assumed someone was the door. Then I explained, I had just gotten into my bed and heard four more knocks, coming from the kitchen area. Since she had heard nothing, I just dismissed it from my mind and thought no more about it. Besides, we had a beach to see, and the town of Mobile, Alabama to explore.

Since this was a condo, a private residence, we didn't have the normal amenities that a person would have in a hotel. That being said, we had access to a washer and dryer, and we had to wash our own towels. We'd been the beach and enjoyed the time around the pool during the course of the day, and we'd done some laundry.

The laundry room was adjacent to the main floor bathroom, so you had to walk past the laundry facilities to enter the bathroom. Either Cathy or I had done a load of towels, and the towels had been transferred into the drier earlier in the day. I knew the towels in the drier were dry and ready to be folded.

I was in the bathroom, preparing to take my shower. As I was in the bathroom, I could definitely hear sounds of footsteps shuffling across the tile floor, sounds, like the washer lid or the drier door had been opened, and closed, with one of the slams that occurs when you are closing the drier door.   I heard sounds as if someone had removed a towel, unfolded it and flapped it in the air to smooth out the wrinkles prior to folding. I just assumed that Cathy was taking care of the laundry responsibilities and thought no more of the sounds that I'd heard. After my shower, I left the bathroom, and I expected to see a stack of folded towels that I could take into my bathroom. No towels were in sight.

"What did you do with the towels you folded?" I asked Cathy once I got out to the living room side.

"What towels?" she responded back.

"I heard you outside the bathroom door, and you had opened up the drier and folded the towels. I heard you moving about in that laundry room while I was in the bathroom."

"I've not folded any towels," Cathy said, with a puzzled look on her face. "I've been upstairs the entire time; I just came down here when I heard the water shut off."

By this time, I had returned to the laundry room and yanked open the door to the drier. It was full of unfolded towels. Cathy was in the laundry room with me, and I said to her, "While I was in the bathroom, I heard footsteps, sounds of the washer lid and the drier door open and close, and the snap of towels being folded. I thought you were folding towels." I then, just looked at her, and slam closed the drier door.

We both walked back to the living room, and I commented again, "I wonder if a ghost is here?"

Cathy tried to make light of the topic and said, "I don't know about a ghost, but I'm definitely hearing things in this condo."

On another afternoon that week, I had plans to go on an gulf excursion and Cathy wanted to remain either by the pool or walk along the beach.   We were both in the condo preparing for our afternoon activities and had made tentative plans for dinner. I also mentioned the time of my return. I collected my items to take with me, and left the condo, with a slam of the door.

Now at this time, I was away in Mobile, Alabama enjoying the attractions of the city. Several hours later, I had returned back to the condo, with thoughts of going out to dinner. Prior to my leaving Mobile, I told Cathy that I would drop her a text so she'd know that I would be traveling back, and she could time the afternoon and be showered and dressed for dinner.

My text was simple, "I'm leaving Mobile now and should be back in about one hour."

Upon my arrival, Cathy wasn't in the condo, which did puzzle me. The text that I'd gotten from her was a simple one, 'I'll be poolside waiting for you.'

I sent her a text stating that I was now in the condo, and to come up on to the unit. Once she arrived at the condo, she was a little unnerved, almost tense, definitely, not someone who had been relaxing poolside or walking along the gulf coast.

She wasted no time asking me, "Did you come back to the condo? For any reason, right after you left. I heard the door slam, and thought you were gone."

Cathy barely gave me time to answer her question. "No, once I left, I got into my car and drove into Mobile," was my response.

"So, you didn't come back here at all? Not even for a quick second?" she asked me.

"No, I didn't. As I said, I got into my car and left town. Why? Is something wrong?" I wanted to know.

"Strangest thing, I was upstairs in the bedroom, just getting my swimsuit and things together.

"I swear, I heard the front door open and close, and I heard, what sounded like footsteps, as if someone was walking around in the kitchen, and then into the living room.

"I called out, '*Robert*' but I heard nothing else.

"I stood still, just listening, but really heard nothing else, so I went back and started getting ready to go outdoors.

"Then it started again, I could hear some movement, again, like someone was walking around downstairs. I called out again, '*Robert, is that you?*'

"Then the movement of the sounds stopped. I just stood still, upstairs, knowing that I was alone in the unit, and that I must be hearing sounds from outside.

"I heard next, what sounded like someone was climbing up the stairs. I wasn't too sure, but it did sound like someone stepped on the bottom step, paused, and stepped onto the next step. And then it moved onto the third step, and it paused.

"When I heard the sound on what was probably the fourth step, I collected my wits and rushed over to the half wall, that created the balcony over the staircase. I looked right down, expecting to see someone, or something, or that ghost, but there was nothing there.

"It was at the point, that I was sure, there was a ghost here, because the sound of the door opening and closing, and movement downstairs, and the footsteps ascending the staircase. Those steps sounded so real, so lifelike, with just the right intensity of a person's weight.

I grabbed my stuff and shot right down those steps. It was at the point, that I decided I would just wait by the pool until Robert returns to the condo.

"Whether there was actually a ghost in the unit or not, I wasn't ready to hang around in the condo to find out.

I just stood there and looked around the unit, trying to imagine a ghost here, or trying to make some sense out of what Cathy had told me. A ghost, possibility, just one too many incidents to just dismiss it as outdoor sounds.

Our departure was the next morning, so we only had one more night to sleep in the unit. When morning arrived, neither of us had anything ghostly to reveal, so it was a quiet night. However, I decided once I get back home, I will contact the owner of the unit, just to satisfy my curiosity.

A couple days later, I placed a call to the owner Betty Robinson, in Birmingham. After the usual greetings and telling her that I enjoyed staying at the condo, I brought the conversation around to some 'unusual happenings.'

At first, Barbara chuckled and asked me to explain. I told her what we had experienced from our arrival at the condo. Barbara was still, in disbelief that a ghost might be in her unit. I told her my background with some investigations and interviews with folks who live in haunted properties, so she started to see some credibility into what I was telling her and asking.

Barbara said she purchased the unit shortly after, 'the love of her life' has passed away. So, her husband had never lived in the unit. Barbara mentioned that I was one of the few people, or strangers, that she has allowed to rent the unit. Barbara said that either she stays in the condo, or her adult children with the grandchildren drive down and use it. Barbara said that nobody has ever mentioned a ghost in the condo, and the children had never said one word about strange things or sounds.

Trying to be tactful and respectful, I asked her if the furniture was the furniture that she moved into the unit, and that if the furniture was what she shared with her husband. I explained to her that possibility, her husband's presence, or spirit, might be attached to the furniture. He'd had no real reason to make his presence known to her, or to their children or grandchildren, however, Cathy and I were strangers to the unit. Possibility, and this is just my reasoning, that her husband saw us in the unit, and just wanted to return to his role as being a protector, the guardian for the true, 'love of his life' as well.

Mercury Ballroom Mysteries

The home of the Mercury Ballroom was built in 1928. Its architectural style is one of a kind, with its use of glazed terra cotta. The building was known as the offices of Wright and Taylor, Inc., a distributor of Old Charter bourbon whiskey. The Old Charter Distillery was located on the northwest corner of 4th and Chestnut Streets, across the street from the Wright and Taylor Building. The building housed small businesses during the prohibition era and through the late 1960s. It was vacant for nearly three decades until the renovated building was opened in 2014 as the Mercury Ballroom.

After sitting abandoned for many years, new life has been restored to the Mercury Ballroom.

The Wright and Taylor Building, at one time, was four separate store fronts. From my growing up and years leading into adulthood, I recall in the late 1970s, a Taylor Trunk Leather Shop at the northern end of the building, a local record store occupying the location on the southern end. Once the record store vacated, a fast food fried chicken restaurant was there, but its time was short. Some older photos shown high end clothing stores for men and women. A Burger Chef (fast food) Restaurant was on the second floor! For many years, the four shops appeared to be nothing more but hollow shells of what was once there. For some of my ghost walking tour business, the front windows were all boarded up, keeping all memories of a time gone by, locked inside.

After doing a little digging, I was able to come up with a little darker history for the building. One source related that it was one time a speak-easy during the final years of prohibition. That's a reasonable explanation since it was at one time, associated with the Old Charter Distillery.

Another source stated that it was used during the gangster era for gambling and prostitution. That's possible as well, since it does have an exit to the tunnel system that's under 4th Street. That would have been a perfect, fast escape for the gangsters.

One source led me to another, and I was able to contact the production manager, of both the Mercury Ballroom and the Palace Theater. His nickname is Scooter, and Scooter says that he's pretty much in touch with things of the supernatural.

"As many years as I've worked backstage in theaters around Louisville and elsewhere, I've had my fair share of ghostly encounters and strange things that can only be explained as ghostly," shared Scooter.

"What's been going on?" I asked him during one of our sidewalk visits.

"Nobody goes on stage without my approval. I work with the performers, the stage crew, sound and audio techs, you name it, I've got my hand involved.

"Sometimes, I think another hand is involved, too.

"Theaters have many traditions, or superstitions.

"One of the best one known by the cast and stage crew, and the one that creates the most atmosphere of all theater lights is a bare bulb called a 'ghost light.' The ghost light is just a lamp that's left onstage when all the work is finished in the theater, and everyone's gone home for the night.

"One explanation is the most practical. Most stages have an orchestra pit, which can be about ten feet below. So, when the power is off, it's pretty dark, but one little globe of a bulb left on, call the ghost light, is for the protection that no one walks in the theater and falls off the stage.

"That's one theory, another one that is more popular is the light is left on because the theater is inhabited by ghosts. The ghost could be of old actors or people who used to work in the building, and ghost lights are supposed to keep those ghosts away so that they don't get too mischievous while everyone else is away.

"Along that train of thought is that the ghost light provides that one lone ghost of an actor, who has faded from the limelight, to be able to step onto the spotlight once again.

"Most of the ghost lights are just simple, slender pole style lamps with a low wattage bulb left burning.

"At a distance, the ghost light seen can look very magical on the dark stage. It's almost like a glow, someone almost floating or alive on the stage, and you never know what ghosts could be lurking around to return to the spotlight, before the curtain goes down."

The Wright Taylor Building wasn't built to be a theater at all, but a business location for the Old Charter Distillery. The walls were all removed, and a stage was established at the eastern end of the building, and in 2014, the doors opened as the Mercury Ballroom.

Keeping with traditions and superstitions of the theater, a ghost light was established.

Now the questions remain: 'Did the ghost light attract a ghost to the building?' 'Or, was the building already haunted?'

One of the episodes that Scooter told me about when we first met, was that a ghost was haunting the lower level of the building. Scooter invited me to tour the building one night after a concert to see for myself.

The lower level has been completely remodeled to accommodate performers with dressing rooms, additional restrooms, a green room, a lounge and eating area.

"It was in this bathroom, that the ghost of a man appears in the mirror!" Scooter said.

I stood in the bathroom facing the mirror and I only saw my reflection. "What else can you tell me about this bathroom and mirror? What happened?" I asked.

Apparently, Scooter wasn't the first to see the image in the mirror. Other employees and talk soon began circulating among the performers about the man's image that appears to be in the mirror.

"I happened to be walking by one evening and I glanced into the bathroom. Something just caught my eye and in that split second, I looked; and I was expecting to see my own reflection, but it wasn't there.

"It was the reflection of a man, who was in shades of grey, staring right back at me!

"I did a double take and after blinking my eyes a bit, my own reflection appeared in the mirror.

"From what I recall, he was in older style clothing, mustache, with some type of a suit coat or jacket and necktie, nothing like guys would wear today."

I asked, "Was it something like from the gangster era of the 1930s?"

He said, "It had that type of a look, with slick back hair. He wasn't smiling one bit, very stern, angry looking, as if, 'what are you doing here?'

"I mentioned it to other employees, and we did seem to have the same consensus on the appearance of the visitors in the bathroom mirror. That man's image really did bother the females who work here. Nobody wanted to be alone down here or use the restroom.

"I've noticed some cold spots in the basement as well, most noticeably by the entrance to the tunnel that leads out onto 4th Street.

"Weird, unexplainable sounds are here in the basement, to the point where I'd think someone was upstairs on the main floor, but the building would be all locked up.

"The most troubling episode occurred in the summer of 2018.

"The city hosted a concert called Louder Than Life, and the Mercury Ballroom was used as a rehearsal space for one, and a place where musicians could just come an crash for a bit.

"It was a late night and I decided to just stay the night here, and sleep on the futon in the green room. I've done it plenty of nights.

"I'd settled down about 2 :00 AM. I heard something, some sound, which caused me to wake up.

"The room wasn't totally dark; some lights were on in the hallway; those lights burn all the time.

"Standing at the foot of the bed, stood the man! He was in shades of grey, full body apparition, staring down at me with this hard, cold icy look!

"I couldn't believe my eyes, nor did I want to believe my eyes! He didn't move, his arms were in a semi raised up position, not as to strike me or anything, but as if reaching for something, and I knew it wasn't going to be me.

"I didn't give him a chance to move. I don't even recall throwing back the sheets on the futon. I grabbed my shoes in one hand and darted past him with both feet flying.

"It seemed like that hallway was a mile long. I reached the door, and something told me to just turn around and look back. A part of me wanted to look to make sure he wasn't following me, and yet another part of me wanted to see him again.

"With both hands on the door handle, and my heart was pounding, I turned back and had one last look at him."

"What did you see?" I asked Scooter.

"He was standing in the hallway, just outside of the door where I was sleeping. What I did notice was his arms weren't raised, but at his side, and he just stared at me, as if he was the one seeing a ghost, something in disbelief in his world.

"He didn't appear to be as gray this time, more faded away around his legs, almost like he was losing energy and was passing back to the grave from where he came.

"I shoved open that door with so much force, it banged against the wall, and that caused me to jump as well.

"I flew up the back steps, which is a fire exit actually, and shoved open the back door just about stumbled out into the alley way. I guess I tripped over something, for I dropped the shoes I was carrying and had to stop to pick them up.

"I stood out in the dark alley, just staring at the now, closed up fire exit door. Carrying my shoes, I walked to the stage door of the Palace Theater, just trying to figure out, what I actually did see in that room downstairs.

"From all accounts, it was a ghost, plain and simple. And a ghost I sure don't want to see again."

"Do you think he would have tried to do you any harm?" I asked.

"Probably not. I'd say he was just as shocked or as puzzled to see me, as I was to see him. My assumption is that he's in a state of confusion, with all the remodeling that has been down to the building and new technology and people coming and going, people that he would have only thought about in the future, not in his time period."

"Do you think the ghost light on the stage has any connection with him?" I asked Scooter.

"I don't think so, but it would just fine with me, if he would stay on the stage and have his time in that light and not in the basement when I'm sleeping."

The Ohio State Reformatory is Ohio's largest castle structure ever built. Used to house the living whose misdeeds and crimes committed brought them here, it has a few restless spirits still serving a life sentence.

Ohio State Reformatory Investigation
Mansfield, Ohio

Two years ago, my sister Robin and I had the opportunity to travel to Mansfield, Ohio, from Louisville to meet up with my cousins. The plan was for us to tour the historic site of the Ohio State Reformatory. We had scheduled a self-guided tour of the building. I had no idea that several movies had been filmed there, including *Shawshank Redemption.*

I fell in love with the building's massive architecture. It looks much like a fortress, which would discourage anyone from the outside trying to break in to rescue someone, or for an inmate to consider trying to escape. Yes, there were some or attempted an escape and a couple who actually made it.

The Ohio State Reformatory is the largest castle like structure that was ever built in Ohio. It stands to this day, as one of the largest structures in the United States. The building has more than 250,000 square feet. The building has towering stone walls. It has the largest free-standing cell block, with is the east cell block, with six tiers.

The reformatory was built as a halfway point for young, adolescent males who were too young to be sent to a penitentiary. The purpose was to teach, enlighten, and reform the young male prisoner. The goal was for the young man to exit the program to be hard-working, well rounded in society, and able to contribute to his world.

Cathy Smith and I had readied ourselves for whatever might come our way for the investigation.

This was one of the last efforts to rehab the young males, and teach them a trade, moral and religious guidance, and hopefully leave as a law-abiding and successful member of society. Sometimes that plan worked, and sometimes it didn't.

I was aware that the reformatory offered ghost investigating tours and I thought, if I was able to go on one, I'd sure sign up. Two years later, my wish came true.

My book publisher, Troy Taylor, and his company American Hauntings advertised that a tour of the reformatory was forming. I wasted no time at signing up.

I invited my good friend and work colleague, Cathy Smith to join me. She was as excited as I was about going to the reformatory. Cathy had never been before, so she was in for a rare treat!

On our particular night, the weather couldn't have been more cooperative. As Cathy and I were leaving the hotel, the rain was pouring down. We were surrounded by thunder, and lightning flashed across the sky.

Driving up the narrow driveway with the massive building before us, we thought the stormy weather set the stage and the atmosphere for our night in the reformatory.

Once we had checked into the tour with the receptionist, I asked to use the restroom. I was directed back outside to an outbuilding. Most of the rain had stopped, but there was still some thunder and lightning in the distance.

As soon as I opened the door to the dark men's room, I could clearly hear whistling. The overhead light was on a motion sensor, so as I continued stepping inside, the whistling stopped as the lights came on. Curious, I looked around the small restroom, and even peeked under the stall looking for feet, which I saw none. I stood in the center of the room, knowing I didn't imagine the whistling sound at all.

Returning to the reformatory and joining the group, I quickly commented to Cathy about my first, possibly ghostly experience, and in all places, the outdoor building for the men's' room.

We went on a building tour first, led by one of the reformatory volunteers named Lonnie. Lonnie loves the reformatory so much, that he commutes from Detroit, Michigan to be involved with the happenings and events. Lonnie was very knowledgeable. We roamed about the cavernous building, down one dark hallway and into another. The walls were lined with wainscoting. A massive staircase was in the lobby. Beautiful, ornate tile covered the floors. Our first stop was one of the original electric chairs that was used at the Ohio Penitentiary in Columbus. The electric chair is on display at the reformatory. The electric chair wasn't used at the reformatory at all. In fact, nobody was sentenced to death there by any forms of punishment like the chair; however, the ghosts of those who did died by other means, for whatever reason, chose to remain.

The construction of the administration and residential side of the reformatory lends itself to a mirror image design. On the opposite side of the administration was the warden's residence. The first floor has 14-foot-high ceilings, the second floor has 10-foot-high, and the third floor has eight floor high ceiling. Not only did the warden reside here, but also assistant superintendent and the chaplain.

The warden/ superintendent was named Arthur L. Glattke, and his wife was Helen Glattke. Arthur Glattke came to the reformatory from his teaching position in Toledo, Ohio. He was appointed the position by the governor of Ohio, Mr. Martin Davey.

"According to the history involving the warden and his wife Helen," began Lonnie, "one Sunday morning, November 5, 1950, as Helen was getting ready for Sunday church service at the local Catholic Church, Helen was accidently shot. Helen was in the bedroom and rummaging through the closet. She pulled out her jewelry box of a locker in the walk-in closet, and a .32 caliber automatic pistol fell out, hitting the floor and discharging.

"The shot pierced her lung. The wound didn't kill her immediately. She was rushed to Mansfield General Hospital and she passed three days later with complications of pneumonia.

"It wasn't exactly clear if the shooting was purely accidental. The rumor started circulating immediately and people started speculating on what might have happened. It was common knowledge that the warden and his wife were having marital problems.

Life at the Ohio Reformatory continued as usual, for the warden, Mr. Glattke, and his two sons. However, that time was short lived. Nine years later, tragedy stuck the survivors of this family.

"On February 10, 1959, Mr. Glattke had a heart attack. He was transferred to the General Hospital, but he passed due to complications of diabetes.

"Now, as for ghostly hauntings, on more than one occasion in the bedroom, visitors get the fragrance of a rose perfume. Just whiffs of it, lingering in the air near the doorway and the closet area have been noticed.

"In the hallway, visitors have reported smelling the faint smell of a cigar, leading visitors to believe that the warden's wife is haunting the bedroom, and the warden, is haunting the hallway."

"Another point in the architectural design is when the sunlight comes into the building, at the center of the building, an X will be cast upon the floor. Skylights and windows are positioned in such a way for the X to, 'mark the spot' as they say in the movies," Lonnie said.

We had just enough remaining sunlight to capture the X on the floor. Some feel a ghostly presence standing here.

On this evening, we were there just in time. The rain had stopped, but enough light from the outdoors came through the windows and we could see the X on the floor.

Our walking tour and orientation led us into the main cell blocks of the reformatory.

Our next location was what was used as the chapel. This is a very large and spacious room with an altar and a painting of one of the saints painted on the wall. The young men housed here attended worship services, with the emphasis of repentance and salvation, instructions of moral living and Bible studies. None of the church pews that are in the chapel are original; however, the thick covering of dust and grit that cover the pews is original to the building.

"Investigators have seen on more than one occasion, an apparition of someone sitting off the side on a pew," said Lonnie.

"Some of these images have been captured on digital cameras and video to prove that it's not just a figment of one's imagination.

"When investigators move over closer, the apparition appears to just vanish, leaving only the trace of an imprint in the dust and grit on the pew, as if someone had just gotten up from that seat.

"Crying sounds have also been heard in the chapel as well, with no source anywhere to be found in the room, or in an adjacent room, or anywhere on the property."

With this private tour, we were able to go where the public doesn't get to go. Lonnie led the group through one of the designated 'No Entry' doors. We crossed over a narrow catwalk, and climbed up a series of steps, with only the aid of our flashlights. We were now, in the attic, over the west cell block. We had dodged rafters and roofing supports, as well as much newer HVAC equipment. A few old chairs were still sitting as if in a conversation group. We passed numerous old bed head frames that were leaning against the walls. We continued walking until we came to the end of the attic.

"Please turn out all flashlights, cell phone lights, or anything that you might have that will light up the room," Lonnie instructed us to do. Everyone complied, and one by one, the lights were extinguished, and the room was at that point, in total darkness.

"The Ohio Penitentiary suffered a great fire, and 100 inmates were transferred to the reformatory.

"Those inmates were housed in this attic. Imagine, rows of beds lined up here, and when the lights when out at night, there were only two or three guards with the inmates, and in darkness.

"Imagine the sounds, cries, shouts, scuffles, uproars, and what little could be done in here? This attic was home to many inmates, some of which, have chosen to remain.

The attic was still in total darkness, and very few noises were made by the visitors on our tour. Occasionally, there was a distant knock, or shuffle of feet off in the distance, or possibly the sound of an old bed squeaking from a bed that wasn't there. Noises, that really couldn't be explained. Lonnie turned on his flashlight and pointed it to an area on the wall. He had highlighted an inmate's name, followed by the inmate's number. On another area that he highlighted, it showed a date, possibly a release date, and another he showed a date, and that date had been crossed out, and another date had been written below it.

"One of the ghosts who has decided to stay was a huge baseball fan. If you want to use your equipment and try to communicate with him, try to engage him into discussing baseball.

"But keep in mind, you'll have to discuss baseball from the 1940s era, not in today's world," advised Lonnie.

Lonnie gave us permission to turn on our flashlights or any lighting devices that we have and to move about the attic. He encouraged us to just walk along the walls and look for names, dates, and numbers. We did see them. Countless names, dates, and numbers of the inmates and most likely, their spirits had remained.

Moving over to the east cell block, it was important that we visit the cell of Mr. James Lockhart. His cell is an active cell for ghostly activity.

"Lockhart was serving 1-15 years for assault with intent to kill. On February 6, 1960, he took his own life by setting himself on fire in this cell with lighter fluid and a match. He was 22 at the time of his death," explained Lonnie.

Several of us gasped and just stood at his cell and looked inside.

"A man actually set himself on fire and died in here," exclaimed my friend Cathy.

We both just stood here in disbelief and trying to picture the tragic scene. I held onto the bars of the cell; Cathy stepped inside.

"James worked in the reformatory carpentry shop. That's how he was able to get some lighter fluid and smuggle it back to his cell," added Lonnie.

We continued walking along the concrete floor, looking up at all the tiers of rows of cells, west side had four and east side had six.

"Eventually, the reformatory administration had a contract for a chain link fence to be installed over the bars, that make up the simple railing.

"Way too many fights were occurring, and inmates were 'accidently' tossed over the side railing and landed hard on the floor.

"And some guys jumped of their own volition, too!

"There's no telling what restless spirts still walk the tiers and catwalks of the building. Some of those restless spirits, went over the railing, over and over again, to meet their deaths!"

One dark hallway leads into another one, almost like a maze, traveling from room to room. All kinds of strange noises echo throughout the building.

On the lower level is the bullpen, where all incoming inmates are met with the guards and the warden.

Lonnie invited several of the guests on the tour to take a position, standing on the yellow line that had been painted onto the concrete floor.

"This is where the warden would speak to the men, and one of his favorite lines to the men was, 'You can give your soul to Jesus, but your ass belongs to me.'

"Investigators who have researched and documented this room, report of being shoved or pushed from the back side, away from this yellow line on the floor.

"Also, just behind you is the entrance way to the solitary confinement block."

Almost walking single file, we went past the heavy door, through arched openings, and past walls of cells.

"This is solitary confinement. Time spend in here didn't count toward the time to be served.

"Tormented souls linger here, men who suffered greatly, and had punishments not only isolation, but punishments of the mind.

"Lights would burn for 12 hours, then it would be total darkness for another 12 hours. The plan was to confuse the normal waking and sleeping pattern, so the guys in here would all lose since of time and date.

"Soon, the men wouldn't know if outside was daylight or nighttime, or if the next meal would be breakfast, lunch or supper.

"Some men did everything they could do, to end their lives in there, or what was commonly called 'the hole.'

"Sounds, moans, cries, are heard from in here, and, of course, when you go to investigate the source, you'll find nothing but empty cells, one after another."

Our tour and orientation lasted about 45 minutes. Lonnie led the group back to the bullpen area, and into a lighted area where we could call our base camp, use the restrooms, enjoy some soft drinks and some food. At that point, we were on our own, roaming about the Ohio State Reformatory with only the light of our flashlight to guide us.

It seemed like most of the folks on the tour scattered and went every direction. Cathy and I decided, since we were at solitary confinement, we'd go back there first.

"It's different, how it looks when it is the light of the flashlight and the two of us walking back here, isn't it? The senses come to life, listening for every sound, temperature change, or imagine that might appear before us," I said to Cathy.

As a courtesy, people spoke in whispered tones and kept their flashlights pointed down to the floor, and not upward to blind anyone. We followed that protocol.

"Shh, do you hear that?" Cathy asked me.

"What?" I responded with.

"Some people are in one of the cells, and just listen; it sounds like that are using equipment to communicate with a ghost," she said.

Stepping as gingerly as possible, we moved along the rows of cells in the solitary confinement area. My flashlight was off so we were moving in total darkness. We only had the sounds of the voices to lead us. As I walked, I used my left hand to physically touch each of the bars of the cells, just as my own guide.

Cathy and I could see on the floor in just a cell or two ahead of us, a faint, red glow light, some type of a power light or some instrument that the investigators were using. Cathy and I didn't make a sound. We didn't want to disturb what was happening, nor interrupt the session of communication.

We could hear the investigators asking questions, 'What is your name? How did you end up in solitary confinement? How long were you down here?'

As Cathy and I stood in amazement, we could hear almost in a whispered male's weak voice, his answers.

Cathy and I looked at each other, the best we could with excitement, knowing that those folks were actually communicating with someone, who was in the cell.

"John," was a whispered voice, followed by, "1947".

Cathy and I didn't make a sound; we wanted to hear more.

"Fighting" and "Almost killed a guy" followed by silence. The investigators continued to ask questions with their spirit of John.

"How long were you in here?" one of the investigators asked.

"Three months," came the weak voice, followed by a sigh, as if it was taking every bit of the energy of the spirit to respond in an audible voice.

Cathy and I stood here, listening, and waiting for something else to happen, but nothing followed. Cathy and I looked at each other and decided to quietly walk past the investigators who had experienced a great session with the spirt of John, the ghost.

Stairwells. Hallways. Catwalks. Narrow passageways all lead about the dark, and cavernous reformatory.

Opening one door, we stepped into what was called the central security area. This large room is where every camera, every piece of security would have been followed closely, as well as the room where visitors for the inmates would have entered.

Inside the large room, we observed three other investigators in a corner of the room. They had their equipment going, and one of the female investigators was having some interaction with a ghost.

Cathy and I stood in the background and listened. I could see the lights of the meters beeping, and the investigators were talking back and forth to each other. An older gentleman in the group had stepped back to where we were standing.

"Having any luck?" asked Cathy.

"We're getting audio recordings of something in the front corner of the room. That's where one of the inmates killed his wife, whom he thought was cheating on him. She had come to visit him, and he had gotten word that she had been fooling around," he told us.

By then, the other two female investigators had come over to join us.

As the five of us stood there, listening to what they had to reveal, the temperature seemed to drop suddenly in a very abnormal way.

"I'm cold all over," said one of the women.

"Look, I've got goosebumps all over my arm, and the hairs are standing up as well on my arms," another woman said.

We all looked down at our arms. My arms were covered in the goosebumps and the hairs were standing up on my arms. I felt very chilly!

"Did something follow us over here from that was in the corner?" one of the women asked.

The watchful eye of Jesus looked at the men living here, and now, looks on at the deceased whose souls have remained in the chapel.

I decided to go up and have a seat in the corner of the room to see if I could detect anything. I took my seat, leaving the others in the back of the room. The temperature in that area of the room was closer to a normal temperature, not chilly like the area that I was standing in.

I sat motionless, staring at the wall. I was able to see a shadow or two moves against the wall. I didn't hear anything, but the temperature did begin to drop. I did hear what sounded like movement behind me, thinking someone else was walking up to join me, but as I glanced over my shoulder, nobody was approaching me at all.

I sat there for a few more minutes, but nothing happened. I stood up and looked back and Cathy was the only one standing in the back of the room. I never heard the others exiting. The other party of investigators had moved on to another location.

We decided to return to the chapel. As large as the reformatory is, we thought that nobody would be in the chapel and we could have some time to be alone, wait for something to happen, and not be disturbed.

With only the light of Cathy's flashlight to guide us, we passed tiers reaching up to the darkness that had cells too numerous to count, trotting on dark, concrete flooring, and through narrow passageways with stone walls. Climbing up another staircase and over a catwalk, we entered the chapel.

An arc appeared in the background by the pew in the chapel.

Nobody was in the chapel, so we were able to roam about undisturbed. I walked up to the remains of the altar and allowed time for my eyes to adjust to the mural on the wall of a saint.

Cathy was on one side of the chapel and I was on the other. I could hear what sounded like footsteps moving about the chapel. Others noises were heard from elsewhere in the chapel. Cathy and I just paused and looked at one another, wondering about the source of the unknown sounds.

I had my camera with me, and at just the right time, I snapped a picture of the pews.

"Look," I said to Cathy, "I got something; a white vapor mist is right over the pew."

The white vapor mist was oblong in shape and appeared as if it were sitting on the pew or rising above the pew.

I showed it to Cathy, and we both walked toward the location that I photographed. Nothing was visible to the naked eye, yet we heard the sound once again, and that was a sound of something rising up from the old, wooden pew, that kind of sound heard in an old church when someone

The doorway to the left of the chapel opened, and some other investigators slipped into the chapel. We exchanged nods to acknowledge one another.

Cathy and I exited the chapel through the back staircase that leads into the administration building.

"Let's go back into the warden's residence and look around," said Cathy.

I was in agreement. We journeyed down a hallway, and past a room that was used in the movie *Shawshank Redemption*.

We were on the second floor of the administration building. We passed nobody as we approached the residence. Rounding one last corner from the hallway and into the residence, Cathy and I both stopped right in our tracks.

"Take a deep breath," I whispered to Cathy, as not to disturb anything or anyone.

"Can you smell it? The cigar smoke is here, just in the area of the hallway, just as Lonnie told us."

Cathy and I both inhaled and walked around a bit more, enjoying the fragrance of the cigar smoke. We walked past the pink tiled bathroom, that was said to be another hot spot for the cigar smoke.

Leading into the main hallway, we found two more investigators with equipment set up in front of three windows.

We acknowledged each other, and I asked if they had been having any luck.

Cathy and I both told them about cigar smoke in the distant hallway.

"Have you been inside of the master bedroom?" I asked the other two investigators.

They hadn't been inside yet, and we spoke of the story that Lonnie told us about the fragrance of rose perfume.

The four of us walked into the master bedroom. It was lit only by the spotlights from the outside that illuminated the building. Our four shadows were cast on the floor.

Then it happened. The fragrance of the rose perfume just filled the room!

"I can smell it," I said to the group.

We all nodded in agreement, that the ghost of Helen Glattke must be present in the room.

The fragrance of the rose perfume was the strongest nearest to the closet. That's the location where the pistol had accidently discharged.

Were the ghosts of the warden, Mr. Glattke, and his wife, Helen, in our presence? Were we seen as guests into their residence this evening and they wanted to be with us? I can only hope so.

The four of us walked about the master bedroom, and even into some of the adjacent rooms, but no cigar smoke or rose perfume was to be found. We parted ways with the other two investigators.

Cathy and I decided to head outside for some fresh air and, maybe, get some tips from some of the others who were outside. Several folks were standing on the side porch talking about their evening.

One of the others asked if we'd been to the Jesus room? Cathy and I looked at one another and we hadn't visited the Jesus room, nor was it a room that was on our tour.

One of the investigators gave us detailed directions throughout the reformatory.

We made it to the Jesus room, which was tucked away into the back of another room. It was called the Jesus room because someone had painted a large portrait of Jesus with his hands outstretched on the back wall. Odd furniture was left in the room, lots of old theater style chairs and dusty tables. From the appearance of the room, and from some photographs we'd seen earlier, I assumed this room was used as a school room for the boys. Several other investigators were in the room, but one by one, they cleared out. That left Cathy and me alone in the Jesus room.

Disturbing sounds were heard in the room, as if someone was walking and moving about on the dirty tiled floor. Furniture creaked as if someone was sitting in the chairs, and the temperature did drop suddenly.

I took some pictures and was able to capture another form of a white mist on the opposite side of the room. Someone was in the room, just as the folks on the side porch had led us to believe.

Cathy and I were satisfied at that point. We'd explored and traveled all over the reformatory and we'd seen, heard, and experienced what the reformatory had to offer for us as investigators.

In the upper corner of the left side a small, white orb had formed. Historians believe this room might have been a classroom.

I'd always heard that ghosts can follow or attach themselves to you. Usually, at the conclusion I just say as I'm leaving, "Thanks for your time, but stay here," because I don't want anyone following me home. I know they can do that. Apparently, I failed to make my verbal statement.

Our hotel lodging was a suite, with two bedrooms, living room, and a kitchen. Cathy had her room and privacy, and I had mine.

I believe that I finally dozed off to sleep around 3 AM, but my dreams were far from restful at all. In fact, my dreams transported me back to the Ohio State Reformatory!

In my dreams of that morning, I was back walking along the tiers of cells and the ghosts were active. The cells doors were opening and closing. Images were materializing before my eyes, of white mists moving back and forth.

Disturbing sounds of cries, moans, and weeping were heard in the dreams. The squeaks of the beds sounded, as if someone was rising from the beds.

Hollowed faced men were appearing between the bars of cells, almost reaching out to me to make contact.

One episode after another continued in my dreams.

Now, either I'd woken up or I voiced this within my sleep, but I recall calling out, "You had the chance to make your presence known, to show yourself, and to prove your existence to me while I was walking about the Ohio Reformatory. Why are you doing it now, when I'm not there?"

"Be gone, go in peace, back to the reformatory!"

At the point, all noises ceased. Pale faced men faded away. Cell doors no longer slammed. Silence and peace, prevailed.

Did something follow me back to the hotel room? Did something decide to become active once I left the property to prove something to me? Do the souls of those men still walk the land and return to the reformatory upon command?

I'll never know, but they did comply with my direction and leave in peace. And from what I can tell, none of them followed me back to Louisville, Kentucky.

Palace Theater's Prankster and Unseen Playmates

The Palace Theater is 90 years old. Several ghosts may still be waiting in the audience or on the stage, for the 'show, must go on.'

In my first book, *Haunted Louisville,* I share with my readers the historical background on the 1927 built Loew's Theater. Today, it is known at the Palace Theater, a name that is very fitting for the architecture gem of the downtown area. I tell the story of the ghost of Barney, the most famous ghost that haunts the building.

I like to interact with my guests and to stimulate conversation. On my ghost tours, guests often ask if any other hauntings have been documented concerning the Palace Theater. I told her yes.

About three years ago, I had on my tour a former employee. This was a young lady named Penny, and she, like many other workers, worked a second job as an usher at the Palace.

Penny was on my tour, and she was excited when I told her that we'd stop by the Palace Theater and I'd tell of the haunting there.

"I'm so excited!" she exclaimed to me. "I work there, and I'll tell you my story, after you tell your story!"

"Deal," I said to her, and her eyes just lit up.

I presented my historical side first and presented the ghost story about the Palace to the audience. It is important that the listeners know the background of any building. Many of my local guests have been indoors of the Palace; it's good to know its past to appreciate its present.

Penny hung on my every word and kept staring at the exterior of the Palace, all wide eyed. I invited my guests to ask any questions, and I encouraged them to take any pictures as we lingered a bit after the story. At this time, Penny came forward and said she had a story to tell me.

I grouped the audience together, and told them that one of our visitors tonight, works at the Palace, and that she has a firsthand experience she'd like to tell. I invited everyone who was interested to just hang around. I could tell she was a bit nervous speaking to a large group, but I knew she'd do just fine.

"I work as an usher here at the Palace," Penny began.

"I work downtown and live too far away, so I don't go home when I get off from work at my full-time job.

"I enter the theater on the back side, down through the alley. There is a door designated for employees to use. I know a couple of the guys who are already down here will have the air conditioner turned on, or the heat. They let me in and I go about my business. Some of the stagehands are here getting set up, but they are down on the stage, not just roaming about the building. Sometimes, it is just me and the security guys here. And I'm usually the only female in the building.

"I bring my uniform inside with me. My black pants, white shirt, maroon vest, and this little necktie. Everyone wears that uniform, both the men and the women.

"Sometimes the lobby is dark, or only a few overhead lights are turned on. Often times, I climb the stairs in the dark to reach the mezzanine level. That's where the restrooms are located. As I walk along the mezzanine, some of the doors to the balcony are open, and I can hear the voices of the workers down on the stage.

"Just as I enter the women's room, I see an antique mirror that is placed over a fireplace. I get caught off guard, when I see my own reflection in the mirror. I tend to jump a little.

"I go into the women's restroom, and I know I'm the only one inside; however, strange things start happening.

"I'll be standing at the sink and looking into the mirror, I can see in the reflection, the doors of the stalls will slowly open, or close. I'll hear the movement from the stall door, and just glance into the mirror, and see a door or two moving.

"Of course, I'll turn around, call out, 'Who's there?" and nobody will say a word.

"I'd go back to getting dressed, something would catch my eye, and I'd just freeze....and sure enough, I'd see one or two of the doors opening or closing again.

"I've heard sounds of feet shuffling about in the room, as if someone is coming out of one of the stalls. I've even stopped and walked around the stalls and looked under for feet for another woman, and no feet would be there! But it sure would sound like someone was in there.

"I've even heard voices, or what sounds like someone would be talking in there. It sounded so real, I'd stop what I was doing and go out into the mezzanine and look around. Of course, nobody would be there.

"There would also be the occasional toilet flushing, or two might flush, and the automatic water faucets would just shoot out water.

"That kind of stuff started to really get to me. If the ghost was there, it was really starting to make me feel uncomfortable. I'd mention it to some of the other guys who were there at work, and they would look at me like I was crazy or something."

I asked her, "How do you deal with it still, going into the theater in the afternoon to get ready?"

Penny said, "I don't deal with it anymore. Now I dress in my car, I found that easier than going inside the theater and get dressed."

Now that is Penny's account of her ghostly encountered in the women's room on the mezzanine level, but that's not the only testimony provided to me for the readers of my book to enjoy.

During my interviews, I was able to speak with a couple of ladies who work in the housekeeping department. Aside from emptying out trash containers that might contain food or beverages, most of the cleaning and custodial work occurs the next morning after a show.

A number of years ago, the Palace Theater opened up passages between the neighboring building, which at one time, was Shackleton's Music Store. Today, the Palace Theater uses this area for receptions, drinks, and concessions. The area can also be reserved, whether it be on the main floor, or on the second level for private events.

I was able to spend some time with Marjorie and Brenda. Both ladies have been employees at the Palace for several years. Both ladies are very happy here, even if a few ghosts keep them company as well.

The ladies began telling me about ghost children!

"What do you mean about ghost children?" I asked.

"On some afternoons, and during the summer, or when school isn't in session, we'll bring our young grandchildren with us to work," said Marjorie.

"We can let the grandchildren run and play all they want to, on the upper level of the old Shackleton's Music Store side. It has a few open balconies so we can keep an eye on the grandchildren from the Palace Theater side. All we had to do it look across the mezzanine from the theater side and see the grandchildren.

"The area that we use for refreshments and banquets, is a large area and we'll leave the kids in that area to play," added Brenda.

"Our grandchildren are small, and I know they like to run and play tag, or such, and run the length of the room."

"One of my granddaughters mentioned to me about playing with a little girl, and she asked me who that little girl was," said Marjorie.

"I didn't know of any other little girl, so I asked Brenda if she knew anything about a little girl to play with.

"Brenda didn't know anything, but she did recall that her own grandchildren, had once mentioned playing with other little children upstairs.

"We'd hear the kids laugh and play games, and just have a good time, and we both just assumed it was imaginary playmates.

"Over the summer or so, the imaginary playmates never went away, and our own grandchildren would rush upstairs to play.

"We got used to hearing the playful noises of the grandchildren. Everything does echo inside the building like that.

"When school started back up, it was just the two of us in here cleaning, and maybe one or two of the maintenance guys. Instead of it being fairly quiet with just us in the building, we kept hearing the sounds of children playing, laughing, and running around.

"Even a time or two, I'd walk back over to that side of the building, just to see if someone else had brought some children in here to play while they were at work, and as soon as I'd reach the area, all the noises would stop.

"This continued quite a bit, and for several months, knowing that our own grandchildren were at school, where was the sound coming from? And why?

"We'd ask the grandchildren about the 'new' playmates, and they'd talk about a little girl, and a little boy, who just hung around the theater and liked to play.

"Of course, these are small children and young children are more perceptive to ghostly images and other paranormal activities.

"But no matter what the children saw, or how they played, we do know that the sounds continued even when the children weren't there."

Brenda agreed with Marjorie when she said, "I kind of miss the sounds of the children when I'm in here all alone. It reminds me that life goes on, and the fun continues that way."

Spiritual Hauntings in St. John's Evangelical Church

In May of 2017, my friends, Jacob and Jenny Floyd, owners and guides of the NuLu Haunted Tours and Shepherdsville Haunted Tours, organized an event at St. John's Evangelical Church in the up and coming NuLu district. This church is hard to miss, with its towering bell tower reaching heavenward. It can be seen from various points of the interstate system while traveling along the elevated roadway. The church has the bell tower illuminated at night, so it really is a stunning masterpiece there at the corner of Market and Clay Streets.

In the Floyds' book, *Louisville's Strange and Unusual Haunts*, the Floyds shared with their readers the history of the church and of

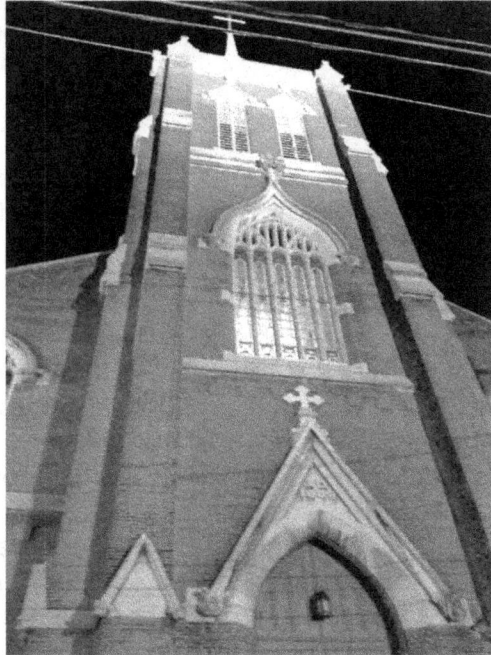

This stunning masterpiece of Christian church architecture is worth visiting for a worship service. There may be more than one 'Holy Ghost' next to you in the sanctuary.

their own investigations. For a more accurate and detailed history of the church, please consider purchasing their book and reading their narrative.

In this case, I was a guest on one of their first public investigations at the church. I will be sharing with you what I experienced on that night. It is important to know some of the history and architectural elements for the story so you can picture the location. I will also detail the events of the paranormal that occurred to me that night.

Jenny and Jacob Floyd, myself, and Kenny Dowell on the investigation.

St. John's United Church of Christ was built by Germans. The location of Clay and Market is the second location. Discussion of the building of the church began around 1860 and the bricks were laid in 1866.

The sanctuary of the church is just a masterpiece of design and art as well. Tall stain-glass windows are on all sides, telling Bible stories and providing comfort and inspiration for those inside. Red carpet lines the pews of the church, and a balcony is across the back for the choir to sing songs of rejoicing. I can only imagine how their voices would fill the sanctuary. The pipe organ is there as well, with its own storied past. The pipe organ didn't exactly make it as planned. The organ was traveling on the steamboat called the *Champion* from St. Louis, and unfortunately, that boat met with misfortune and sank. A replacement organ is in the loft today. It is said that some of the pieces of the original organ were excavated and have been returned to the church.

We had one of the church's representatives to serve as our historian and guide, plus one other elder was present to answer any questions. Autumn works at the church as a secretary, and a PR person, plus she works with bridal parties who wish to use the church. A gentleman from the church, whom I will refer to as Mr. Wilson in this writing, was also present to provide a historical background, and to answer general questions about the church, the ministry, and ghosts, too! Autumn was the first to announce that the property is haunted! She's been employed here for many years, and from early daylight to late night hours, Autumn's been there with ghosts to keep her company. Mr. Wilson didn't confirm or deny any ghostly activity, but it was apparent, he was happy to be with us on this night of investigation.

I had invited my buddy Kenny Dowell to come along. He brought along his own video recording devices, hoping to capture something ghostly.

Even though this was an organized ghost investigation led by the Floyds, we had freedom to move about as we so desired.

The church and two other buildings were open for our inspection. The church is where we all first met for our initial orientation presented by Autumn and the Floyds. For the rest of us in the group, we did brief introductions of ourselves and backgrounds. Next, we traveled as a group into the parsonage, and the church elder, Mr. Wilson, provided us with some background on the parsonage. The final building that was available was the Parrish House. We walked over

The parsonage has a feeling a love and comfort. Is that the one who caused the lacy curtains to move when the house was empty before we stepped inside?

there and gathered in the rear fellowship hall to hear the history and usages of this building over the years.

Once we had the initial overview of the properties, we knew where we could go, and had heard stories of what had been observed that was ghostly. We were free to move about at our own leisure and to follow our own instincts or impulses.

Kenny and I left the Parish Hall and decided to start our exploration in the parsonage. Autumn had left the Parish Hall and was headed there. The minister's home is a two-story, red brick structure, with large windows across the front. Some furniture remains in the rooms on the main floor. The parlor on the left side of the house is a large, spacious rectangle shaped room. Several of the rooms on the main floor are used for bridal party groups in preparation for weddings held in the church.

Visitors would enter the parsonage from the back side. Four steps led inside, and this is a shelter area with a roof, creating a porch like location. Two windows are on the back side, next to the exterior door, and one more window that would be from the kitchen. Jenny spoke up with excitement in her voice. She said to Kenny and I, "The lacy curtains in the back window just pulled open, almost like someone was inside looking outside! Nobody is inside the house!"

We stepped inside the first room. This would have been a dining room, and a table, and other dining room furniture are still placed in the room. From this side, we walked over and looked at the window. I did notice and HVAC vent on the floor, however, but Jenny clarified as to what she saw, the parting of the curtain wasn't due to the A/C blowing cold air. As Jenny described, this was like a hand had reached between the curtains and pulled the left panel back. Cold air blowing from an A/C vent would have caused both of the curtain panels to sway to the opposite side, and this wasn't the case. As Jenny now demonstrated to us, it had to have been a hand parting back the curtains.

"Robert, would you use your dowsing rods, just to see if you get any type of activity or response?" Jenny asked me.

I pulled out my rods and walked about the room asking general questions as if a ghost was there. I was also curious as if the ghost that I was trying to make contact with, was a female resident of the former parsonage. "Is there a ghost here? Do you belong to the parsonage? Where you happy here?" I asked as I moved about the dining room table hoping for a response.

Standing still and near the window that had the curtains that moved, I steadied my hands. I could feel the rods being pushed into the open position. I felt confident that the ghost in the room was a female. I'm not sure if it is a ghost from the parsonage or not.

I decided to set the rods on the table and pull out my camera. Without any hesitation, I snapped a picture, but not necessarily thinking I'd capture an image. I just wanted to document that window and location.

To my astonishment when I reviewed the picture I rushed over and showed it to Jenny and Kenny. A large, white oval mist was right on the curtains! Something was definitely there, and it was a large enough of a form to be seen. Just seeing that form, thrilled us and stirred excitement into us as we ventured elsewhere into the parsonage.

Kenny and I joined up with Autumn and another female guest in the living room of the parsonage. The room has some furniture, so it does look like a livable room, even though nobody lives there. I snapped a couple pictures, but to my dismay, I saw nothing in the pictures. I moved about the living room, just taking in the room, and wondering about all

Within minutes of starting, I captured this white arc moving in the dining room of the parsonage.

the events that had occurred in this room. I noticed, that through the doorway and into the hallway on the western side, a staircase leads to the second floor, and if someone continued up the stairs, that staircase will lead to the third floor, or attic. The living room was lit with a few table lamps, but the hallway that has the staircase, only had the natural, outdoor sunlight penetrating the few windows and the glass in the front door.

I asked, "Has anything ghostly been reported to happen in the living room?"

Autumn spoke up and moved about the room. "Not exactly, other than a feeling that something is in here, like someone is watching every move you make. At least, that's what some of the brides and bridesmaids have said to me.

"Something has been seen trying to materialize itself in the hallway staircase. It seems like something is trying to either ascend the staircase or descend the staircase."

The doorway was open that led into the dark hallway, so I went to investigate, leaving the others in the living room. The window's shade was pulled down, and the glass window in the front door was obscured from any natural light from penetrating the doorway.

Kenny joined me for a second in the hallway, and then he stepped away. He told me that he wanted to go explore the basement. Autumn and the other female guest remained in the parlor and were discussing the furniture and any relations to the families that lived here.

I walked along the hallway, with the wooden floor creaking beneath my feet. I passed the countless, carved bannisters that descend the stairwell. I noticed that the house still had all the dark woodwork that was so popular at that time. The front door was closed and well secured, and it appeared that it has been a long time since it has been opened.

I stood at the bottom of the steps and looked upward, being very curious as to what was upstairs. I like to take photographs to document my time, so I positioned my camera to shoot upwards.

As I looked into the viewfinder to make any needed adjustments, I couldn't believe my eyes. Sure enough, as I pressed down the shutter, I could see a white formation of something trying to manifest itself! The white formation took on an oval shape and just moved at a rapid pace across the staircase from left to right, then quickly descended the staircase. All this occurred within milliseconds, all within just that flash of time it appeared, and it was gone! That white form faded from sight as it neared and traveled down the staircase near me. I was just about stunned, and I turned around to see if anyone was standing near me who could have witnessed that little bit of paranormal excitement.

Nobody else was around. The others were still in the living room, so I was all alone in the hallway to witness this act. I quickly went up to the second floor, hoping that whoever that was, or whatever that was, had returned to the second floor and others would be present.

The second floor was a collection of bedrooms that had experienced several years of negligence. Most of the rooms were vacant of any furniture, and it had been a long time since any real housekeeping or maintenance had occurred up here. It was like time had stood still.

The parsonage had a second staircase near the kitchen. Kenny had come upstairs using that second staircase, whereas I traveled the front staircase. We met in one of the back bedrooms. I told Kenny what I had witnessed and described it to the best of my recollection. I asked Kenny if he had recorded anything in the upstairs or in the basement, and unfortunately, his answer was no.

Autumn had mentioned some paranormal happenings in the back, northeast bedroom, but as Kenny and I moved about in the room, trying to pick up anything, or communicate in any way, nothing happened. If anything was in the back room, the energy level must have been very weak.

Kenny and I decided to go into the Parrish Hall next door to the parsonage. We exited the parsonage from the back side and walked to the adjacent building. The entrance led us into the larger fellowship hall for the church membership to use for meals or gatherings.

Our guide, Autumn, had commented that most of the readings, or activities occurs up on the second floor in the auditorium. We walked the main floor to the front of the building of the lobby. Two main staircases were on each side of the lobby, with a wall, almost like a ticket booth in the center. Chandeliers hung down. Upstairs was the auditorium. According to the history of the congregation, the church was known to produce annual plays called the Tom Thumb Productions. We did see some older photographs taken from the 1920s and 30s of the production, with cast members, parents, and folks in the audience. Apparently, this church was known for this form of entertainment, and must have been a huge event. Children were involved in this production and most likely performed in the starring roles.

This auditorium was located on the second floor, and that appeared that time had stood still when the final curtain on the stage closed. Stepping inside the auditorium, I noticed two or three other investigators moving about with their equipment on the extreme left and right. On the stage appeared to be silhouettes of other investigators trying to make contact with a spirit box. All these investigators moved about, speaking in whispered tones. I'd never seen wooden folding chairs that made up the seating in the auditorium. The wooden folding chairs were all connected together in groups of five for folks in the audience to use. Dark chandeliers hung down from vaulted ceiling. The stage was at the far northern end and I was standing at the southern end. With the rectangular shape of the room, the vaulted ceiling, and the exterior light from the outside, cast shadows all over the room. This atmosphere really created an illusion of a very long room. The traditional looking, black and white tiles, faded from the years marching on, covered the wooden floor. To the sides were some smaller rooms that were just used as storage now. Kenny had moved into the smaller rooms to the side with his video camera.

I walked down the aisle and reached the stage. I noticed a couple other investigators, Jenny Floyd, and another lady in a smaller room, a room that most likely was a dressing room. This room had four steps that lead to the stage. I had my dowsing rods with me. I went upon the stage and had my dowsing rods in my hands. I moved about the one remaining backdrop that was left leaning against the back-stage wall.

I'm definitely a novice with using the dowsing rods, but I still enjoy them and tend to get excited when they work.

I started out by asking simple questions. "Are children here? It is okay, if you're here, just let me know."

With each gentle step I took on the stage, I continued asking questions. "Did you perform in the Tom Thumb Play?   Did you enjoy the sound of applause?"

Step one, steps two and three, to stage right and stage left, I'd move and ask, "Are you alone? It is okay to push open the dowsing rods. Let us know you are here."

By then, Jenny, Kenny, and some others were standing along the proscenium stage watching me as I tried to communicate with any presence that might be there. "Do you miss the glow of the spotlight on the stage?"

I could feel the tender pushing of the dowsing rods being moved to the open position. "I can see it moving," whispered one of the other investigators in excitement.

"I can see the shine of the outside light, hitting the dowsing rod just right, creating a shine, or a reflection," another one of the investigators added.

Looking down at the group gathered at the edge of the stage, I said, "With each question that I asked, I could feel the pushing of the rods moving into the open position. Whatever the spirit is, a child or adult, it is very weak. It must not have a lot of energy, but its presence is with us. Most likely the ghost has returned to this stage. This stage must be its connection."

None of the others were having any positive results with their investigations. Jenny had her spirit box, but it wasn't providing much communication back to us. We could hear a few sounds, but it was difficult to make out clearly what was being communicated to us. Kenny wasn't getting much on his video. After several walks throughout the upstairs room, Kenny pushed the pause button. As a group, we decided to head over to the final location of our investigation, the church.

Kenny and the others walked around to the back entrance of the church to reach the sanctuary. I felt compelled to walk around and view the church from the Market Street side. I noticed the gothic doors and thought of all the people who passed into and out of the church over the decades. I stood out front, staring up the massive bell tower. I could see that the stain glass windows had some light illuminating from them. Leaning back and staring up at the church tower, I felt like any traffic or noises from pedestrians had all faded from hearing. The tower just held me captive. I knew I wanted to go to the top, and nothing was going to stop me. If the church was haunted, I knew the ghosts would be there!

Everyone else had gone inside the church. I walked in the dark, between the parsonage, and the church to reach the back entrance. With each step, I stopped and stared up at the windows of the parsonage. Then I'd turn, and stare at the stained-glass windows.

I was the last to arrive inside the sanctuary. Several were standing at the altar while a few others were making their way to the vestibule. One of the members of our investigation was from Louisville Ghost Hunters. He had set up several cameras in the main sanctuary, vestibule, and the balcony. He had several computer monitors on his table, with plenty of cables and cords stretched all across the red carpeted area.

As we grouped around his tables in the vestibule, he explained to us that he had been recording any activity that was occurring in the empty sanctuary. He had replayed some of his videos back to us, and we could see white, mist like images moving between some of the pews of the church toward the altar. He switched to another monitor and showed us what he had recorded from his camera placed in the balcony. In some of the frames, a white mist, almost like a form of a person, had manifested there. He said either Autumn or Mr. Wilson had named the ghost of the balcony Mary.

A ghostly presence was photographed in the balcony, near two other investigators.

Standing the vestibule, I nudged Kenny and directed his attention to the wrap around staircase that led upstairs. "I'm ready to go up," I said to Kenny, and he nodded in agreement of, "Let's go."

I was so eager to climb to the top. Kenny, and a couple other investigators followed us to the balcony. Several of us took seats in the balcony, but not together or in close proximity to one another. I took my seat and just started snapping pictures. When I paused and reviewed my pictures, I noticed that where two other investigators were seated, that they weren't alone. A white mist, or shape of a person, had joined this couple and was seated behind them.

From the balcony, it is possible to ascend another staircase to an upper floor level. From that area, about four or five steps led past a door, a door that appeared to be concealed in the paneling of the wall. Several of us wasted no time and climbed those steps, which led us into the lower level of the bell tower.

This particular area of the bell tower, appeared to be about a 14x14 square room, with to one side, a rickety old ladder. The Floyds were there, and two or three others with the investigation. I knew what Kenny was thinking, and he wanted to climb the ladder as much as I did.

Kenny and I steadied the ladder as we started the ascent. From the top, we passed through a square opening, that led us to the next level. This put us on the opposite side of the large, green and amber stained-glass windows that I saw from the outside of the church on Market Street. A large rope hung down from the wooded plank ceiling that was above us. On the floor was a large, plywood sign, that was covering an opening in the floor on which we were standing.

I read out loud, "Prayer Healing Service" and I motioned for Kenny to help me slide over this sign. The sign was covered in dust and grime, and what was once painted in white with red letters, was almost difficult to really read.

"I'd say it's been a long time since this sign was placed out front, inviting people inside," I said to Kenny.

This sign was found in the bell tower covering a trap door.

Kenny and I slid the sign to another part of the floor, which revealed the folks who were standing down on the lower level, and they were looking up at us.

I started to snap a few pictures of this area. After several pictures, I reviewed my pictures. The air was calm up there, almost to the point of being stuffy. But, when I reviewed the pictures, I could see many large orbs appeared to be rising from the open area, where Kenny and I moved the sign.

"Look at this," I called to Kenny.

We looked at the pictures where there were no orbs. Yet, in the next couple pictures, the large, gray orbs were centered right over the opening in the floor. "It looks like to me, that once we moved the sign, these orbs were now set free."

One remaining ladder waited for us to climb. This ladder had a couple of the steps missing, and this ladder was fairly steep. As I mentioned, my plan was to climb to the top, and sure enough, I carried it

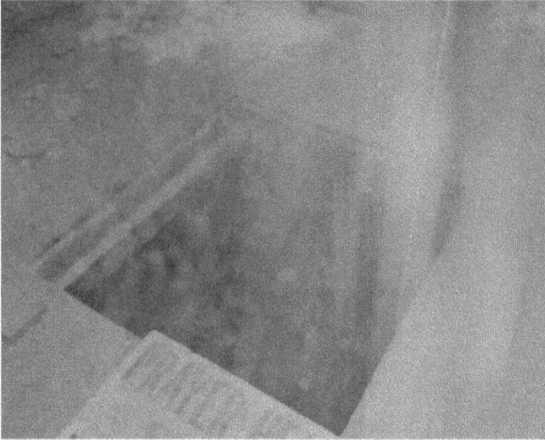

Did we release something ghostly?

out. Reaching the summit, I peered through a dark opening and broke through the cobwebs. I saw the bells of the church hanging there.

Descending to the next level, Kenny and I continued our own investigation. I was still thrilled with the orbs from earlier. I snapped some more pictures and this time, I saw in the pictures what appeared to be a gray fog, or mist.

"We're definitely disturbing something that is haunting up in the bell tower," I commented to Kenny. He agreed as he continued to move about with his video camera.

We continued moving downward to reach the others, who had waited on us at the bottom level of the bell tower. I shared with them the pictures that I'd taken of the orbs coming from the opening in the floor when the sign was moved, and the gray fog mist as well.

Almost one by one, each person left this area, and descended down the stairs that led us back to the balcony. Kenny left, and I was alone in this room. I couldn't help but to look upward, into the tower to see the construction of how it was built. Something just impressed upon me to take at least one more picture before I left this area.

I turned and with just a quick snap of the shutter, took one picture. When I reviewed the picture, I couldn't believe my own eyes. In the photo was this cylindrical, bright white form. It was tall, with some white fading at the top, but bright white as it reached the floor. It didn't quite touch the floor; it was almost as if it were floating! It had no arms or legs, just a solid mass of bright whiteness.

I hurried down to show Kenny and the others. I descended those stairs, and once I reached the bottom, I paused, and turned and looked back into the room. I saw nothing with the natural eyes, and I knew it was there. I stepped over, and since I was the last one there, I reached up and pulled the cord to turn off the light. Since I was standing at the bottom of the steps, I then reached up and closed the door. Thinking to myself, that whatever that is in there, it might want to remain in there and be at peace because we were all visitors to his location.

Whatever is in the bell tower, can remain. It only puts that spirt, closer to heaven.

I was the only one that was still upstairs. All the others had left the balcony and had descended the staircase to the vestibule. I could hear their voices of conversation as I went down to join them. I was quick to show them what I had captured with my camera and how it played out. Maybe the ghost just wanted to make its presence known to just one person, and that one person was me. Some of the others wanted to go back up there and investigate, but I told them that I'd turned out the light and closed the door. Of course, they were welcome to go back upstairs and investigate, but they appeared to be satisfied with what I had to share with them.

And I was satisfied too!

Stewart's Dry Goods Department Store Ghostly Designer

Most Louisvillians have some connections to the long-gone, famed department store that once held a prominent place at the corner of 4th and Muhammad Ali Blvd.

My mother said, "My Aunt Corrine purchased for me a teddy bear from Stewart's when I was a little girl. I loved that teddy bear! On another time, my Aunt Corrine took me shopping for a new Easter dress. I don't remember what the dress looked like or what she paid, but I remember being in the store and have the saleslady dress me all up. When I got a little older, my Aunt Corrine and I had a meal in the Orchid Room Restaurant. Those are some of my memories of that grand department store."

Stewart Dry Goods was the place to be, be seen, and speak of in conversation. Many fond memories for people, to this day and writing of the book, still speak of the Stewart Dry Goods Company.

Another friend, Roberta chimed in that with her memories that "Stewart's was like shopping in New York and I always felt important."

In Louisville's early retail days of the 1800s, the Retail Merchants Association listed three major department stores, J. Bacon and Sons (1845), Stewart (1853) and Kaufman-Straus (1879). J. Bacon's opened in 1845, and Louis Stewart's New York style stores became the benchmarks for all other retailer outlets to follow. Stewart's first location was at 4th and Jefferson in 1853, and the store made the big move with a massive construction project, anchoring the corner of 4th and (Walnut) now Muhammad Ali Blvd in 1907.

The magic of Stewart Dry Good hasn't totally faded away from the memory of Louisvillians. Today, the building has been repurposed as an Embassy Suites Hotel.

The impressive, seven-story building known at Stewart Dry Goods, opened with 62 departments of quality merchandise, tearooms, bakery, restrooms, doormen, and elevators with elevator operators, this New York style of shopping was truly a destination.

Some of my earliest memories of Stewart Department Store were the Christmas displays and window shows. I recall going with my parents on cold December nights to stand outside and look at the Christmas decorations of the Santa Claus, the trees, and of course, all the toys.

As the economy and times changed, so did the fanfare of Stewart's. During the mid -1980s, the flagship store closed its doors and sat vacant until April of 2015, when the Embassy Suites and Hotel took possession. Long gone were the customers exiting through the revolving doors with packages in hand, and the multiple windows that once held the latest fashions and Christmas displays, were layered with dust and grim from the city streets.

In the fall of 2014, on one of the ghost walks, I had on the tour a former employee of Stewart Department Store.

"Stewart's was the only job I ever had!" Marion began. "I worked for 30 years there, and I loved every minute of it. I was in the ladies' shoes department mostly, but it was such an exciting place to be, and yet, it was a sad day when word came that the store was closing. That's when I knew, it was time for my retirement. It was such a glorious time period in my life. Stewart's was the place to be; that's for sure. I started at the store in 1955, just right after I graduated from high school.

"Of course, all kinds of ghost stories circulated about the building of the owner, Louis Stewart. You know how the building was large and cavernous with lots of back storage rooms and staircases that only employees would have ever used. Employees used to speak of Louis' ghost and some of the tales just gave me the creeps.

"It was so easy to mistake a ghost and it simply turned out to be a mannequin in the dimly lit stock room. Everyone would chuckle at that.

"But the one story that still comes to mind, revolves around an employee who worked there in the 1950s. I never knew her, but her name and story were told over and over again.

"Her first name was Jane, and I can't remember her last name at all, and people would just say, 'Jane the ghost' and everyone would know.

"Back in the 1950s, women didn't hold high jobs of leadership, but Jane, from what I always heard, was different. She had worked her way up to be in charge of advertising.

"Jane was an artist, and at that time, Stewart's advertising wasn't of models and photographs, but an artist drew the models and the models looked so fashionable.

"Jane was pretty popular and very talented. She'd lend her talents to helping design the window displays and setting up displays in the store.

"Jane and her husband had marital problems. I don't remember exactly what the squabbles were about, but I'd heard it had turned violent.

"In the 1950s, women didn't have many options like they do today. Shelters were unheard of, plus there was the stigma of a divorced woman, and believe me, people were quick to point fingers and make blame. The most used blame was, 'women belong in the home' and if she were at home, that marriage would have worked. It is easy for people to make assumptions like that.

"The story was that the marriage turned bad, very bad, and Jane sought refuge here in the store. Believe it or not, management protected her after she left her husband and went into hiding here. Jane lived here in the department store! Up on the seventh floor, some rooms that had been converted into a private little apartment that became her new home. I'm sure it wasn't anything special, but just some rooms with plumbing that had been dedicated for her privacy and a place to call home.

"The department store is a public building, and her husband could walk into the store anytime he wanted too, and he did. He usually didn't have any problem tracking Jane down.

"Whenever the husband would enter the store, word would circulate among the employees and let Jane know that he was here.

"On more than one occasion, those two met in the store, and heated words were exchanged between them. The husband demanded that Jane return home, which she refused. On some occasions, it turned violent. The husband would hit her, or he would grab her by the arm, and he'd jerk her, leaving bruises! Some of the male customers would hear words being exchanged and intervene, just like some of the men who worked here.

"The most hurtful altercation occurred up on the seventh floor. He had managed to follow her into the workroom where she did her drawings, and eventually, into her apartment. Male employees discovered the two having words and had to separate the two during the struggle. Security was called and the husband was just about, physically man handled and tossed out the back door of the store, down on the loading dock, and told never to return, or else.

"The husband, not wanting to take no for an answer, returned once again. This time, he was met with security and some men of the store. And after that final confrontation, he was never seen again. "Some say that he was tossed down the back stairway and out onto the loading dock.

"A number of days passed, and Jane acted more normal and things were back to business as usual. Advertisements were being printed in the newspaper and the window dressings and displays were up for each sale.

"In fact, the husband just kind of, disappeared. The few times Jane was questioned about his whereabouts, she would just smile or just brush off the questions, with general answers of, 'he's out of town,' or 'he's gone to visit his mother' and then just change the subject. It was obvious that Jane didn't want to discuss the matter any further. As far as Jane was concerned, he was out of the picture and that suited her just fine, until his ghost decided to return and make his presence known on the seventh floor.

"Jane continued to live in her secret apartment, and she kept to herself. She'd make plans that once she gets back onto her feet, she'd move out of the store. She finally moved out once the ghost started to haunt the building.

"Maybe the ghost of her husband hurried up her departure from the store. Maybe his ghost was trying to torment her as he did when he was living.

"Employees began to have sightings, and to hear noises as if a scuffle was happening. Soon, employees just didn't want to be up on the seventh floor alone at all.

"One employee would report seeing a male figure up on the seventh floor, that would be seen darting around the boxes of merchandise. Some employees would see the dark figure, become alarmed and leave the area. Some would return with security or call for some of the male employees that someone was in that area, lurking, looking, in the area of the artist room or near her apartment. Men would go investigate but find nothing there.

"Another employee would speak of hearing sounds that would be heard, much like a struggle was occurring behind boxes or racks of dresses. Heavy footsteps of men's hard sole shoes against the wooden floor, women's heels as if she is running would be heard, but nothing would be seen. But, when people would go to find the source, nothing would be found as evidence that people had been there.

"Could that ghost that would terrify employees up on the seventh floor, be the ghost of Jane's husband who just mysteriously disappeared? Nobody knows for sure.

"Once Jane left the store and her apartment had been cleared out of her personal belongings, it wasn't totally the end of the mysterious male ghost. His ghost was still haunting the seventh floor, and his presence was seen. Employees still made reports of seeing the male figure around Jane's former apartment and in the back area and stock rooms.

"Maybe once he came to the realization that Jane wasn't there anymore, he saw no more of a reason to linger and wait for her to have a final confrontation... or try to persuade her to come home for the last time."

On my investigation there, I was invited down to check things out, and see what I could come up with. My guest, Cathy Smith and I were provided with one of the newest rooms on the eastern side, on the 7th floor. Arrangements had been made with management to allow me to have full run of the building, from the roof to the basement. We had as our guide, one of the nighttime security guards, Pam.

Pam spoke of just unexplainable things that have occurred while she was at work. She shared with us the shadows she had seen, strange sounds, and how objects would be moved or found elsewhere.

Pam allowed us to use one of the few, remaining, almost untouched back staircases that led from the roof, to the basement. The staircase had the decorative, wrought iron railing and marble steps.

I had with me my dowsing rods. I've had them for a number of years and like to use them on investigations. It is a simple tool, used by holding the rods steady and balanced, then ask a question. If the rods swing open, that is a yes answer, if they cross over, then the response is a no. I saw this as an opportune time to try to communicate with any spirits that might be lingering. I explained how the rods work to Pam and my Cathy Smith.

I asked the general questions of, "Is there a spirit here?" and the dowsing rods did respond in the yes or open position. Pam and Cathy's eyes opened wide. I continued my inquiry with a few more general questions of, male or female, harmless, former employee, and if you are happy here. All of the responses came back as yes responses, and I did encourage Pam and Cathy to use the dowsing rods and ask questions when they were ready. Both of the women accepted the invitation to do so, and asked questions. They both exclaimed that they could feel the rods moving or being pushed into the open response for their questions.

The spirit seemed to be harmless in nature, but each response grew weaker and we waited longer in duration for the answer. Eventually, the last question I asked, had no response whatsoever, so I recommended that we call it a night for our investigation in the stairwell.

Our investigation continued up to the seventh floor, where the story of the Jane and her husband would have played out. I used my EVP meter and got slight responses as we walked the hallways, passed empty hotel rooms. No particular area revealed a strong presence, other than the eastern side of the 7th floor, where, Jane's workroom and apartment would have been.

Was that the ghost of Jane or possibly her estranged husband, whose spirit or spirits were still lingering?

Could it be, or some other spirit haunting the building after all these years? But our investigation was stimulating as well, just trying to piece together, the sordid and violent tale of Jane and her husband.

The allure of Cumberland Falls attracts the living and the deceased to return.

Stirred by the Moon Bow at Cumberland Falls State Park

Who doesn't love a big, bright full moon? I never grow weary of gazing up to the dark sky and searching for the different phases of the moon. The full moon is the form that I find most exciting. Does the full moon really make people do strange things?

One of my most full moon memorable experiences happened a couple fall seasons ago. When I'm telling the stories for Louisville Ghost Walks, one of my locations is a dark and narrow, downtown alley. I tell of the ghost of a man who was murdered, and his spirit haunts the alley. On this particular night, all the conditions were just right. I was leading my guests on 4th Street, and I had to turn from 4th Street into the alley and walk east. Between the five-story building on my right and the two-story building on my left, past the taller parking garages and high rises in the distance, just overhead, was a perfectly round full moon. It couldn't had been placed more perfectly to light up the alley for the telling of a ghost story.

As the title conveys to the reader, Cumberland Falls, which is the main attraction for the state park, located in southeastern Kentucky, is not too far from Corbin and Williamsburg, Kentucky.

Cumberland Falls is a 60-foot drop water fall of the Cumberland River. It flows at a rapid pace between hills and mountains, ridges, gorges, and past gigantic boulders, racing and crashing below. At one time, tourists could walk on a wooden deck behind the Falls. That route has since been destroyed by the forces of nature, never to be explored again. Tourists to the park stand at various overlooks to enjoy the rushing river water and the majestic Falls plunging downward. Just the roar of the Falls itself is almost mesmerizing. During the day light hours and the sun is in the best position, a rainbow in all the colors is visible. It's easy to hear tourists oohing and ahhing at the site of the rainbow. Excitement fills the air.

On nights when the moon is full and the sky is clear, another great natural phenomenon happens on those night. It's referred to as the majestic Moon Bow. The Moon Bow occurs only in two places of the earth, Cumberland Falls, and Victoria Falls, South Africa. When viewed under the right conditions, the naked eye can see the arc of a moon bow, and the shades will be in the ghostly white hues. The moon bow is formed when light, reflected off the full moon, is refracted like a prism in the mist of the Falls.

Locals and employees do feel like on full moon nights and when the moon bow is visible, the ghosts tend to come out on those special nights.

Daredevils have tackled the falls in kayaks and canoes, and some drownings have occurred as well. Some folks were lucky to be rescued and lived to tell the tale, while others become the ghostly spirits that call the park home.

The ghosts that I'm going to introduce to you and not all associated with tragic deaths of the Falls, but men and women, young and old, whose lives were cut short by various reasons, some still unknown to this day. They have remained to make the park their homes for all eternity.

If DuPont wasn't able to visit the lodge while living, I surely hope he has made some visits as a ghost.

On the night of my visit for my interviews, I decided to visit on a full moon night in expectation of the moon bow. My room reservation had been made for one night at the DuPont Lodge.

The DuPont Lodge was constructed in the year of 1934, and has 26 rooms, a lounge, stone fireplaces, a lobby, kitchen, and dining room. The lodge was named in honor of T. Coleman DuPont, of Louisville for his generous gift of the funds to purchase the land for the state of Kentucky. Nobody knows for sure if DuPont ever visited the lodge, and this was due to his untimely death in the city of Louisville. However, it is believed that if a male ghost did haunt the lodge, that it would be DuPont himself. None of the employees denied sensing the presence of a male ghost, but none of the employees that I spoke with had ever seen any resemblance of a male ghost in the lodge. Most agreed, it's just a feeling of a male in the main building.

Cumberland Falls has an age-old ghost story of a young bride and her groom. The bride met a unfortunate death way too soon. This story has been passed on for generations. What makes this different is that I was able to speak with a park ranger who did witness the apparition.

An accident occurred in the 1950s. A young couple who had married were honeymooning at the Falls. They had reserved a cabin. They decided to visit the Falls and explore more of the park.

Since the wedding festivities were in that afternoon, and all the guests had departed, neither the bride nor the groom bothered to change from their wedding attire. They decided to go for a walk.

They stopped near the point of the Pillars that overlooks the Cumberland Falls. It is a scenic look out that tourist have a very panoramic view of the Falls. The groom wanted to take a photograph of his beautiful bride with the Falls in the background.

The bride was posed way too close to the edge of an 80-foot drop. In her excitement of being a new bride, she danced and twirled about full of merrymaking. She moved way too close to the edge and then she slipped and fell to her death.

The rushing waters of Cumberland Falls carried her body away, never to be seen again.

The area that she fell, is now known as 'Lover's Leap' due to her disastrous fall.

Since she fell wearing her wedding dress, her ghost is seen as a young woman dressed entirely in white.

The road leading down to the Cumberland Falls parking lot is very curving and a steep road. Some drivers have exclaimed that while either ascending or descending the road, it's almost like the front of the car will touch the back of the car, with the hairpin curves. The road itself would challenge the most skilled drivers.

Motorists have slammed on their brakes at the sight of a young woman darting about the road wearing a long, white dress. She is said to make appearances on the nights of the moon bow.

During my visit, I was able to meet one of the senior park rangers, a man approaching retirement from the state parks department, named Al.

During my visit, I was able to meet Al, one of the senior park rangers, who was approaching retirement from the state parks department. Al is in his late 60s, and he was wearing the traditional green and khaki ranger uniform. He joined me on the patio overlook of the DuPont Lodge. We had a wonderful panoramic view of the Cumberland River from an elevated area on the hillside. The roar of the river could be heard echoing between the hills, all the way up to the patio on the back of the DuPont Lodge. He was happy to speak with me about this incident that occurred to him.

"I was traveling back to the lodge late one night. With all new safety regulations in place, a park ranger is responsible for locking up the gates that have access to the Falls at midnight. I was driving in my jeep and had reached the middle section of the curvy road.

The fireplace in the lobby of the DuPont Lodge has been the location for the ghost of a little girl.

"I'm sure you know the road; it is just one S curve right after another one until you reach the top.

"All of a sudden, a female, dressed in white, darted across the road. I slammed on the brakes and stopped the vehicle. At first, I thought I'd struck the woman with the jeep, but with the aid of my powerful light flash, and as I scanned the roadside, I found nobody there.

"The road is too narrow and with solid rocks on both sides. It would be impossible to turn around safely. I had no choice but to ascend to the top of the steep incline and turn around in the lodge's parking lot. I had radioed to any other available park employee to race to their vehicles and descend the hill and help me search for the mysterious woman I'd seen and thought, I had struck.

"Several park employees in their jeeps and personal vehicles descended the hill. Some pulled onto the shoulder of the road, while others blocked both the bottom and top of the hill to prevent other vehicles from traveling in either direction.

"We searched the area, but found no trace of the woman seen.

"She was dressed in all white, like a robe or a gown.

"She ran in front of the jeep, almost coming from out of nowhere. Her eyes had this dark, hollow look to them. I thought I'd hit her!

"I stopped immediately and with my flashlight, looked all about. I kept the lights of the jeep turned on, but they only lit up the solid rocks," ranger Al said.

"She was not to be found, that is, if she was among the living; but I don't believe she was," I commented.

Al and I continued talking and we had walked into the lodge's lobby. Hardwood floors, a massive stone fireplace is at one end, and the true, rustic feel greets the visitors in the lobby area.

"At the lodge, I do feel that if a male ghost would be haunting that property, it would be the ghost of DuPont himself. That's just my personal feeling of hauntings," I commented to Al. He did agree with me on that.

I was introduced to Brenda, who was working behind the desk as a check in clerk. Brenda spoke of an encounter that another former desk employee, Theresa, had told her about. The other employee, Theresa, wasn't available for my interview since she no longer works there, but Brenda spoke on her behalf.

"Theresa was working the desk one night. The lodge was pretty quiet with only a low number of guests occupying rooms. Theresa said nobody was in the lobby at the time, nor in any of the adjacent meeting rooms off the lobby.

"She looked up and saw a little girl standing by the fireplace! She was in shades of gray and just danced about the fireplace, pulling on the hem of her dress as she twirled about. "The little girl looked at Theresa, smiled, and took off running around the corner of the fireplace. She darted right down the side staircase, and toward the guest rooms of the lodge.

"The little girl was so far down the hallway, and she almost just vanished into thin air.

"Other desk employees have spoken of seeing this little girl, and she's always by the fireplace dancing about.".

I asked, "Has she been seen elsewhere in the building? Have any guests reported seeing a little gray girl dancing about?"

"No, only the few employees here. Nobody has mentioned ever seeing her elsewhere in the building, and no guests has mentioned it either.

"Now, this isn't related to the little girl, but awhile back, I was working the night shift. I had a couple come down, complaining about all kinds of heavy foots steps, noises, talking that's going on in the room above them. They weren't mad, they just wanted a new room that didn't have guests overhead.

"Sometimes it is just easier to move guests who want to be moved than to try to solve a problem with noisy guests.

"I said it wouldn't be a problem and I'd be happy to put them in a new room. I found them a room on the third floor, thinking that would be best and they'd have a restful night's sleep.

"The husband and wife stood there, telling me about the footsteps, loud talking, almost like a party atmosphere and commotion going on in the room above them.

"I listened, smiled, and nodded as they were detailing to me all they had heard.

"I asked for their room number and key card, and when I looked down, I realized they were already in a third-floor room.

"Glancing onto my computer screen, I noticed that the room they were occupying had no neighboring guests, and since the lodge only has three floors, it would be impossible for a raucous to be going on above them. The attic would be above the guests, and no employees would be in the attic at night, and definitely not having a party there.

"I knew I wouldn't be able to convince them otherwise, so I gave them the key to another third-floor room and away they went.

"Since the lodge had been built and added on in sections, maybe they were hearing something that was going on, and that something had to have been unnatural."

Brenda told me that I need to stay up tonight, and talk with the third shift worker, Cathy.

Around midnight, I returned to the lodge from viewing the famous moon bow at the Falls.

As soon as I walked into the empty lobby, Cathy was quick to ask me if I'd seen the moon bow.

"I'd seen part of the moon bow on the left side, and part of it on the right side, but unfortunately, I didn't see the full arc. However, a gentleman was next to me with high tech camera equipment and a tripod. He showed me the pictures that he was able to take and in the LED window, I was able to see the full moon bow, complete with the arc," I told her.

I asked her name and told her that I was told by Brenda to speak to Cathy about ghosts. The woman behind the desk was Cathy.

"Oh, I believe in ghosts," she said excitedly.

"I believe this place is haunted, and for me, strange things always seem to occur around the 3 AM time period."

"How long have you worked here?" I asked her.

"At least six months, and I've always been on the third shift schedule like this. So, I'm the night owl of the lodge," she said.

"What makes you think the lodge is haunted?" I wanted to know.

"Some of the rooms just give me the creeps. I have to go around and make sure all the exterior doors are locked, which isn't creepy in itself, but there are two rooms that I have to go inside of. I hate securing the Magnolia Room. I feel like eyes are watching me in there, so I hurry inside, check all the doors, and leave. I will purposely leave the doors open with the door stops in place, and as I walked from one end to the other, something closes the door!

"You've probably heard of the ghost of the little girl. I've seen a glimpse of her, or it was a ghost of something. She was by the fireplace. I saw one shadow of something in the hallway that leads back to the guest rooms.

"The craziest thing of all, happened this past Easter. Let me show you what I'm talking about."

Cathy came from behind the check in desk and we walked over to the massive stone fireplace. Since I was visiting in July, shortly after the 4th of July holiday, the mantle was decorated in the colors of red, white, and blue, with ribbons, flags, and other seasonal items.

The mantle appeared to be about six-foot-high off the floor. It seems to have a width of six or seven feet across. It was constructed of stone with a slight edge around the mantle.

"We had all kinds of Easter decorations on the mantle, little rabbits and chicks, lots of the bright green plastic grass for baskets, and large, plastic, colorful eggs.

"The rabbits and chicks, and little daffodil flowers were displayed on the edge. The animals could all stand up. The large eggs were in the back, by the wall, sort of blocked by the green plastic grass.

"I heard the clock strike at 3 AM, three chimes. I usually don't jump, but I did this time.

"Something caught my eye and I turned and looked at the mantle.

"One of the Easter eggs, somehow, rolled through the plastic grass, and past the rabbits and chicks, without bumping into or knocking anything over.

"The egg falls to the bottom of the fireplace hearth, and it keeps on rolling. Now look, this hearth has a raised stone edge going all the way around, to prevent the soot and aches from scattered. The egg didn't stop.

"It went over the stone edge, rolled onto the hardwood floor, and somehow, it had enough force, to roll up the fringe edge of the carpet. It continued rolling about two more feet onto the carpet," explained Cathy.

Standing there, I looked down at the floor of the fireplace, and yes, it has a raised stone edge. I bent over and felt of the rough stone hearth. About one to two feet of hardwood flooring is next, then about two more feet onto the carpet, so the egg appeared to have rolled four or five feet from where it landed.

Logic would have the egg stopping once it hit the stone flooring of the fireplace, and the raised stone edge would have prevented it from rolling further. Even if it did go over the raised stone edge, what kind of force would have kept it in motion on the wooden floor, and what strength could have caused it to roll over the fringed edge of the carpet and to keep going?

Cathy and I just looked at each other. She added this, "When we took down the Easter decorations, I had told the other employee about what happened. Since nobody else was around, this other girl and I purposely stood up on a chair and rolled an egg to the edge of the mantle, to see what would happen. We rolled several eggs, and each egg hit the stone floor of the fireplace and just landed there and stopped. Or if it did roll further, the raised edge by the floor of the fireplace stopped the egg from rolling any further.

"Some unseen hand, something, pushed that egg that distance!" Cathy said.

Cathy just gave me a smile and shook her head, like she was still wondering what happened with the Easter egg.

Time has stood still, within the walls of the Falls Gift Shop. Is it any wonder, that ghosts have remained here?

I had no explanation to give her.

The next morning, I was due to check out. I ran into a couple other employees in the lobby. Brenda was working and she asked who I'd met the night before. Brenda was with the park naturalist, Brett. He was standing there listening and chiming in with what he'd heard as well, about the ghost of the little girl. Brett recommended that I go down to the gift shop and speak to the ladies in there. I'm glad he did, those ladies were helpful and full of information.

I drove down to the gift shop area and parked. I had to walk a short distance past the roaring Cumberland River. I could clearly see the waves bouncing and crashing into large rocks. This area welcomes the tourists and is the main entrance to all visitors to reach the Falls and the overlooks. The gift shop is on the left, and at one time, a coffee shop was across the way on the right, but today it is more a natural habitat museum of animals and history of native peoples. This little area was built in 1952, and very little has been done to change its stone appearance and brown trimmed windows with multiple panes. Glass vases and trinkets are displayed on shelves in the windows. Native flowers were blooming out front. Large windows are on both sides of the gift shop, so visitors can see the museum and the river from the inside windows looking out.

Reba and Candace were working that morning in the gift shop. Reba has been the manager for 16 years and Candace has been employed for eight years. I considered both ladies to be knowledgeable on the area, legends, history, and ghosts.

Reba was involved with clerical duties at first, but Candace was available.

"I don't like to go into the basement," started Candace.

"The stockroom is there, and so is the office, and restrooms.

"Not only is it creepy, but I've heard footsteps while being down there.

"One time, I thought another employee, Ginny, was down there and trying to play a trick on me, and she was making the footstep noises. I even called out, thinking Ginny was there playing pranks, 'You're not going to scare me!' and come to find out, Ginny wasn't down there. I was alone."

Reba was now available, and she joined in the conversation.

"Remember that time you were at the cash register and something touched you on the shoulder?" asked Reba to Candance.

"Oh, yes," said Candance with eyes wide in excitement. "I thought it was another employee, but something put its hands on my shoulders."

"I could feel them, so real, but as I turned, nobody was there. At first, I thought someone needed to pass by me and was excusing themselves for bumping into me, so I didn't feel any fright. But once I realized nobody was there, that made me feel a little frightened. I didn't like that sensation!"

"I've been here the longest of anyone," said Reba. "Things happen at random times of the year; however, it seems like more things occur in the winter, and that's probably because we have the fewest customers in here during that season.

"Crash sounds will be heard, and I'll go look to see what fell, or what tumbled down to create that crash sound. But I'll get to the area where the sound seems like it came from, and nothing is disturbed. Everything is in good shape.

"Voices are heard, mostly mumbling sounds as if people are talking about things, and I'll look up to see if they need help or any assistance. Nobody will be there. But I know what I've heard, and that was people talking," said Reba.

I thanked the two ladies for their time and for sharing the experiences. Neither lady seemed to be too disturbed by sharing their work location with ghosts.

It's anybody's guess as to who these restless spirits might be. The spirits could be age old people from an ancient period of time, and those spirits have decided to remain observing at the Falls, listening to the roar of the never-ending churning waters, or waiting for the Moon Bow to make its appearance once again.

The Church's Unholy Spirit

One of the great perks of leading Louisville Ghost Walks is the opportunity to meet new people and to hear their stories. Back in October of 2017, at the conclusion of my ghost walks, a taller gentleman, mid-40s wearing a Demin jacket over his Mountain Dew tee-shirt, jeans, and black Vans sneakers, and his wife, with dark, shoulder length hair and a welcoming smile, wanted to share an experience with me.

"My name is Darryl, and this is my wife Nancy. We loved your tour! I'd like to share something with you, if you have some time.

"Would you believe that the church where I work is haunted?" Darryl began.

"Ghosts are found everywhere and, in every culture, even going back to the Bible times, so I'm not surprised," I said to him. "What makes you think it is haunted, anyway?"

Darryl removed his wallet and handed me his business card with the church's name and address on it. I wasn't familiar with the Baptist Church that was printed on the card.

"It's not an old building. The church was built in 1950, so I'm assuming the ghosts that haunt it are from former members who were there when the corner stone was laid. If you're interested in doing an investigation, or at least coming to the church to hear my story, I'd be happy to show you around," he said.

"I'd love that opportunity, so when my ghost walks are over for the season, I'll be in touch," I told him.

We shook hands and exchanged contact info with our cell phones. I waved them both goodbye and thanked them for joining me on the tour. "I'll be looking forward to seeing you in November," I said.

We scheduled a time in November. I had no problem finding his church, located on the outskirts of Jefferson County. The church was situated in a smaller, residential neighborhood with a few, neat and well maintained, red brick houses scattered about. I pulled into the lot and admired the stain glassed windows. An educational building was built in the back of the sanctuary. It appeared to be at least three stories high. The sign for the office was posted at the door.

Darryl met me at the back door, and introduced me to the associate pastor, Joyce. They led me up the staircase and into his office. I felt very much at ease, with Darryl's casual attire of Levi jeans with a chain was his wallet dangling down his leg, tee-shirt and maroon high-top Vans. I sensed this wouldn't be a stuffy, formal interview being on the church campus. The associate pastor, Joyce, pulled a chair and joined us. I noticed a collection of Darryl's photography on the walls, a bookcase full of leather-bound books, and a large window that looked out to the grounds.

"I've been working here as the office manager for the church for about four years. I do whatever needs to be done, such as general maintenance, locking up, answering the phone, bookkeeping, or helping with the members in any way that I can. Joyce helps out with clerical work. We both, including my wife, we all give of our time to work with the children and the youth of the church, and the neighborhood. Everyone is welcome.

"Let me show you around a bit, and we'll talk about ghosts, or spirits, or whatever might be the best term.

"Follow me, and I'll take you to the first place where something strange happened to me.

"I was just walking down the hallway, the very same hallway you walked down, heading into the room that was to later become my office space. I had just walked under this light, positioned here in the ceiling. The lightbulb just exploded! Bang! Shattered glass, sparks, you name it. I stopped short, looked up in disbelief, wondering what in the world caused that light bulb to just 'explode' like that.

"Joyce and I have both heard this, and it's the sound of someone walking in the hallway. I'd stop, and go look into the hallway, and nobody is there," Darryl said.

"I've heard the walking sound as well, and even in the stairwells, as if someone is going up and down the steps," added Joyce.

She pointed to the staircase where the footsteps have been heard.

"Shadows have been seen in the hallways, just like the footsteps are heard. Often times, it is the sound of the classroom doors slamming shut, and I'm the only one in the building, and Joyce and I will just stop and look at each other. Something's here."

The three of us stepped back into Darryl's office. I couldn't help but admire all the accessories and conversational pieces he had scattered about to reflect his unique personality.

"If you'll notice this one wall, it just doesn't look right," he said.

"I agree. What's wrong with it? How can you mess up a wall?" I joked.

"It has a slight bow formation up against the exterior wall," he said. "The room isn't necessary in proportion with how this window is centered and the door. By that I mean, the rooms directly above us, are mirror images of what is on this floor. Four rooms upstairs, and four rooms down here on this level. The room above us, is of a different size, and it doesn't have that wall there. Yet, this room has this wall, and it was installed at a much later date.

"Something about this wall, its position, and what's on the other side of it, remains a mystery.

"I've got a friend who's in the ministry. He stopped by the church to visit with me one day, and I was showing him around.

"We just stepped into my office, and the first words out of his mouth were, 'Dude, what's wrong with the wall?'

"My minister friend walked over, looked at the wall, and touched it, rubbed his hands over the surface. He turned and looked at me and by now, all the color had washed out of his face. He said to me, 'Something evil is on this wall, or within this wall, or trapped behind this wall.'

I rose from my seat and walked about and rubbed my hands over the surface of the wall.

"Keep in mind," said Darryl, "my minister friend had never been inside of here before, and he came to that conclusion. Something impressed that upon him!

"I've covered it with some of my favorite photographs of my family and my travels, that makes me feel more comfortable in here.

"My attention always is drawn to the wall. I've often wondered, what was the reason for it, and what's on the other side of the wall?

"That same visit, with just my friend and I in here, we both heard what sounded like someone walking down the hallway. Since the office door was open, we just turned toward the door, thinking someone might come into the room to say hello. I knew better. I knew no real person was walking here, but my minister friend didn't. I knew all the exterior entry doors were locked!

"We both saw the shadow of someone pass in the hallway. But nobody was there as a real person. Just the shadow.

"My friend just felt like praying for peace and serenity in the building, so he moved about the room anointing and placing his hands on the door frames and up against the wall.

"One Sunday morning, we were having a senior Bible study in the first room, at the top of the steps. You passed it, as we walked to my office.

"My wife Nancy, Joyce, and me, plus about five or six of the senior citizens, were meeting in there.

"My wife and I heard it first, and that was what sounded like a dog barking, or growling in the building. Then, Joyce and I exchanged looks, she had heard it too. Since the three of us heard it, we never said a word, thinking, the others didn't hear it.

"The senior citizens in the Bible study did heard it, but nobody commented, until it got much louder and it couldn't be ignored.

"Somebody's let a dog in here, as a joke or something,' one of the members blurted out.

"I tried to downplay it as much as possible, thinking to myself, I'd heard weird sounds before in here. But they wouldn't let it rest but wanted to go investigate.

"Oh, it's a dog outside, or kids playing, maybe someone has their music up too loud, I told them, but none of my excuses satisfied their curiosity.

"I knew the doors were all locked, and we were the only folks in the church at that time. I knew it wasn't a dog, and really tried to discourage them for going on the search of the building. But they insisted.

"We all divided up and set out to search for the dog, that was supposedly in the building.

"One of the oldest guys in the class, had walked down the hallway. Joyce was right behind him. He turned and started to walk into my office.

"At that time, I had a fan sitting up on the desk, and the fan was placed right in front of the window. Next thing I knew, all this commotion broke out! The fan, almost was lifted off the desk, became airborne and flew across the room, just narrowly missing landing on the man's feet.

"We all came a running, and that flying fan really did startle the man. There was no way that fan could have lifted up, and flown, possibly ten or more feet across the room, without some serious force causing that to happen.

"No dog, or any animal was ever found in the building at all. The noises, the barking sounds, all just stopped at that point.

"That wasn't the last of the noises, they did return."

"What happened next?" I asked.

"One evening we had some children and youth activities here in the building. We keep the upstairs rooms off limits, so the young people have to stay in the fellowship hall and in those adjacent classrooms for their games.

"This one little fellow named Willie was quick to tell me that a little girl in a red sweatshirt had slipped off, and gone upstairs.

"With this building, two stairwells are on both ends of the hallways, so I knew Willie didn't see any such little girl in a red sweatshirt. Nobody had been here wearing a red sweatshirt, but to satisfy Willie, I told him that I saw her come back down the other staircase that's at the opposite end of the hallway.

"But I knew better. It was a ghost that Willie saw.

"Sometimes, I get the feeling, that something must be lurking in the empty rooms upstairs, and it might want to try to lure up the unsuspecting children there.

"That little girl in the red sweatshirt might have been that ghost, with the intention of trying to get another child to come upstairs, with the plan of playing with her. However, something a little more sinister might have been wanting, and that's what concerns me.

"Another reason why we keep all children and youth almost confined to the fellowship hall. They don't need to be upstairs at all."

"I agree with you," I replied.

"On another occasion, my wife was doing some painting in one of the hallways. She said something came up from behind and shook the ladder she was standing on. But, as she turned around, nothing was there.

"One of the volunteers was helping out in the kitchen. I was standing not too far from her, and something reached up, and lifted up a strand of her hair! Her hair lifted almost straight up! Hair just doesn't do that!

"The hallways and some of the other rooms had the typical cold spots, and even strange smells. Some of the strange aromas remind people of cigar smoke, or whiskey, or more unsettling, human or animal waste! Where in the world would that odor come from?

"One Sunday I was giving some announcement prior to the church service. This ringing sound, like an old school bell was ringing. A couple of us just looked around, since it was such an unusual sound.

"Two of the men got up and went downstairs. The bell ringing stopped. I kept on with my announcements and scripture reading.

"When the men came back upstairs, I asked what they discovered to be the source.

"I knew this bell was there. It's in the fellowship hall, high up near the ceiling, and it looked much like a school bell that would ring. We've not used it in ages. It was probably used as a signal for Sunday School, or to conclude classes, but we've not used it. In fact, the switch on the far wall is covered with black electrical tape to prevent anyone from flipping the switch.

"However, when the men went to silence the bell, they discovered something pretty unusual, almost creepy. For whatever was supplying the power that was causing the bell to ring, remains a mystery, because no electricity serves that bell. The wires were severed a long time ago!

"The bell was removed from the wall.

"The most troubling and almost scary, is the sound of a growling sound! It comes from the kids' playroom in the basement.

"This sound has been heard often times when the kids are gone, and a few adults are left in the building. We'll hear it! That deep, growling sound, almost sends chills down your spine.

"It's pretty intense, really scary sounding, a noise that would make you stop in your tracks and look around, or at least, over your shoulder.

"I wouldn't necessarily endorse this action, but a woman in our party that night decided to challenge it, or whatever was making that growling sound.

"She went into the kids' playroom, and the sound, the growling sound was at the far end.

"She walked to that end and tried to confront it. The rest of us joined together in prayer.

"When she returned, she had the strangest expression on her face. Her eyes were wide open, and she had the strangest of a smell. Her body really had a foul odor, that just couldn't be explained. She didn't act right, and she didn't elaborate on what she saw or heard.

"We didn't hear any more of the growling sounds.

"But back to the basement, the kids have mentioned seeing shadow people moving about, and adults have mentioned seeing the same apparitions as well.

"One little fellow, who went to see it, said that what he saw looked like a vampire!

"This fellow took off running as fast as he could, and he kept on running even outside. Whatever he saw, a shadow or the vampire, just about scared the living daylights out of him

"Now here's where it gets odd. As that little fellow as he was running from something he saw, his leg bent in some unnatural way!

"When I saw him with the leg bent, I just knew he'd broken a leg! But no, he got up and was fine. Something just scared the daylights out of him.

"Another one of the kids from the youth group was in the basement and he was kicking around a soccer ball.

"He said that he heard a voice from behind him say, 'Kick the ball, do it again.' As he looked around, nobody was there!"

"Would you say that whatever this holy spirit is, haunts the entire building, that no place is actually a safe haven?" I asked.

"I'd have to say, we do have those safe haven rooms, where nothing has happened. We had room with a children's sandbox. Inside the sandbox, we have some prayer stones. The other room where nothing has happened has been the prayer chapel. Those two rooms are really peaceful for adults and the children."

"I'd say this is a pretty active building," I commented to him. "Whatever is haunting the church might just want to make its presence known, but they are going in a pretty dramatic way.

"Maybe one day things will calm down. As I've told folks before, a haunting might not necessarily be the building itself, but possibly the land."

"Unless it wants to reveal itself, you, your wife, and the associate pastor, may never know what's going on here." I said.

Several weeks after my visit, the opportunity came up for me to visit the church on a Wednesday night. I'd been in contact with Darryl, who suggested a night that would be good. We agreed upon a time that the children and youth activities would be over, and only Darryl, his wife Nancy, and Joyce would be there. It would be a good time to just be alone in the church and explore the property on my own.

I arrived onto the church property after the sun had gone down. Only a few lights were on inside of the property. Only two cars were parked in the lot. Joyce met me at the door and welcomed me inside.

Several of the overhead lights were turned out and the church was quiet. Nancy was in the fellowship hall putting away some of the refreshments that hadn't been eaten.

"Has anything happened here, since I last visited?" I asked.

Nancy and Joyce had joined me at one of the tables in the fellowship hall. "The only thing that I've heard has been the strange noises and footsteps," began Joyce. Nancy nodded in agreement, that has heard them as well.

Darryl opened the door and came downstairs. He had just returned from driving the van and dropping off the few remaining children.

I asked Darryl the same question, if he'd experienced anything from my last visit.

"Nothing out of the ordinary, such as noises and footsteps in the building," Darryl replied.

"Do you mind, if I just roam about the building on my own? I'd like to keep things as normal as possible, that way, if you all need to do anything to wrap up your evening services, I don't want to be a hindrance. Also, I want the ghosts to just be as active as it wants to be and not see me as a threat of a stranger or anything like that," I asked.

I was given permission to explore the entire church on my own. The others gathered up their things and said that they would be up in the office upstairs.

My first stop was the children's playroom, a large area were games were played with the children and youth. I walked about the room and voiced to any ghosts that they were welcome to make their presence known to me, and that I meant no harm whatsoever.

For the most part, the room was clean and orderly. I could smell a fragrance of flowers, thinking that a custodian had just been in the building that day.

I took several photos with lights turned on, and with lights turned off in this basement room. In one photo, I did get a white arc of light move across the view finder.

I went upstairs to the sanctuary and moved about, from the back end, to the front pulpit. I even stepped onto the choir loft. None of my instruments reacted, such as my dowsing rods or my EMF meter. I did my best to encourage some activity. This was room that was well maintained and spotless, and in certain areas, I could smell the fragrance of the flowers.

In the educational building, I climbed the staircase to the 3rd floor, and snapped several pictures. I did see one faint orb in the hallway. I didn't hear any footsteps, or shadows, or anything. I did step inside of the prayer room and did sense a level of peace.

One of the Sunday School rooms had been cleaned out and was empty of all furniture. It was in this room that the senior citizens thought they'd heard a dog a number of weeks ago. Other than the room being empty of all furniture and the slight fragrance of flowers, I got nothing in my photography, my dowsing rods, or my EMF meter.

Time was passing on, and since I wasn't getting any activity, I decided to meet up with my church host and hostesses and call it a night. I didn't want to keep them there any longer than necessary, and since nothing was responding to my requests for activity, I thought it best to just call it a night.

The churches' office was on the second floor, and as I came down from the 3rd floor, I could get a few whiffs of the fragrance of flowers. The only footsteps that I heard were my own as I walked to the church office. I could see their light turn on in the office, and the hallway overhead lights were out.

I met up with Darryl, Nancy and Joyce. "Did you get anything? What did you think?" were the questions they asked.

"Unfortunately, I got nothing but one little arc and one small orb. I heard no footsteps, no shadows, no noises at all," was my explanation.

"I'd say that the building is clean, so if anything is here, it has chosen not to make its presence known to me. Something that just happens.

"I do want to give my compliments to the housekeeping staff, the whatever the air freshener or cleaning supplies, in several of the rooms and hallways that I visited, I was greeted by the fragrance of flowers.

Darryl, Nancy and Joyce, all turned and looked at me in almost disbelief as to what I had said.

"Fragrance?" they commented.

"Yes, the flower smell throughout the building. It was almost like the fragrance of flowers were following me, what type of cleaning supplied do you use here?" I asked.

Darryl spoke up, "We only use Pine-Sol! None of our cleaning supplies are floral scented at all! And in fact, that's one of the fragrances we smell in the building, flowers!

Nancy and Joyce, both agreed that they have smelled flowers in the building when there was no way that floral scent would be in the building.

"Do you think, something was following me about the church, and it was creating the floral scent?" I asked.

That was the best explanation we could come up with. The two ladies agreed that they have smelled the floral scent, however, Darryl spoke up and gave a new perspective.

"I've not smelled flowers; what I smell is something pretty bad, offensive like, almost like human waste in the building. But I've never found the source at all, just a bad smell.

"That's definitely not what I was smelling; it was the flowers," I answered back.

Since it was getting late, I decided this would be a good time to just say goodnight.

I exited the office on my own, and I could find my way to the exterior door. The parking lot was dark, and my car was parked just a few empty parking slots away.

Once my foot hit the pavement, my EMF meter just went crazy, with the beeping sound. I stopped and pulled out the meter and the needle was just flying back and forth. I was shocked, it never reacted to anything while I was indoors, but now, it is going crazy with the beeping sound. I did walk about the brick exterior, thinking I must be picking up some overhead wiring or something electrical. But, as I looked upward, there was nothing connected to the building.

I opened up my car door, while the EMF meter was still beeping.

As soon as I sat down in the seat of my car, I pulled the door closed. I hadn't even inserted the key car into the ignition...and then I smelled it.

The interior of my car was filled with the same fragrance of the flowers, the very same scent that I had smelled inside of the church.

Whatever was following me inside, had decided to join me in my car. I started the car and began driving off the church property. Within seconds of leaving the church property, and fragrance of the flowers soon faded away as well.

The Gate House's Ghostly Visitor at the Water Company

For the three summer months, different historical buildings in the city participate in what they call, 'Walking Wednesdays' and that is just a fancy way of hosting a free, open house for people to come onto the property, and tour.

As a Louisvillian, I'd never been onto the property on Frankfort Avenue, known at the Louisville Water Company.

Peaceful and serene from the outside, ghostly activity on the inside. Could it be a ghost of a male employee from long ago haunting the property? Or possibly, a ghost of a female paying him a visit?

Countless times, I'd driven down Frankfort Avenue and turned my glance up to the scores of runners and walkers, getting their exercise on the deck of the water reservoir.

Since my scheduled allowed for this visit, I decided to drive down Reservoir Avenue and visit the Gate House, a Gothic structure built in 1879, that I'd only seen in pictures. Now was my opportunity.

I didn't anticipate anything ghostly from the building, but I just had the feeling, that if it wasn't haunted, it should be! I walked along the tree lined sidewalk, and climbed the two, massive stone staircases to reach the landing.

The doors opened to the Gate House at 11 and I arrived around 11:20. A handful of visitors were already there, milling about the outside, along the deck, or pointing to the ducks swimming in the water. I walked

Looks like a perfect place for a ghost, but I didn't feel that the ghost or that woman would have ascended this staircase in that dress.

in the front door and I stopped at this large barrel to pick up a bottle of water.

From my peripheral vision, I saw a woman standing in the corner of the building. I noticed and nodded to acknowledge her. She was dressed in a Victorian long blue dress, high collar, white lacy covering, and her hair perched up on her head, but she never acknowledged me or nodded or anything in return. Her hands were clasped in front of her. I turned to the left to see a display from across the room, and maybe took two or three steps, and turned back around, and she was gone!

In those few minutes, my mind just processed the woman as being a docent, in period clothing to help set the mood. The woman did seem to have a blank expression on her face, almost staring off into space. But, with me, it all happened so fast, and she looked real, so I didn't stand there and stare at her.

But I thought, how did she get away from me so quickly? I'd only moved two or three steps at the most, and the main entrance door is right behind me, she would have had to pass behind me to exit the building. She still puzzled me, and her blank stare and posture continued to weigh upon my mind.

I walked about the building on my self-guided tour, I kept looking for her. I ruled out that she'd climbed that cast iron staircase with the long dress, plus I ruled out that she was outside in the heat, but where did she go?

I still wasn't convinced she was a ghost, until I had a conversation with the only two employees in the Gate House. Only two water company employees were there, Jay and Barbara. When I noticed that Jay was alone and not preoccupied with other guests or brochures, I just causally struck up a conversation.

"Where is the woman in the Victorian blue dress? I saw her when I first walked into the Gate House, and with her dress, she'd look good in my pictures," I said to him.

Jay had this real puzzle expression on his face, "What woman in a blue dress?"

He didn't know what I was talking about. I shared with him, that when I entered the building, I saw a woman, standing in that corner, the one I pointed too, and said she was

The woman that I saw was standing in this area. Is this a haunted corner with some significance to the building?

standing right there in a blue, Victorian dress with her hands clasped in front of her.

Jay just scratched his head, and just looked at me, and said, "I've not seen a woman like that in there this morning, since we opened the doors."

Jay motioned for the other employee to come over, and he introduced me to Barbara. Jay directly asked Barbara about a woman wearing a blue Victorian dress, who I'd seen standing in the corner. Jay asked her if she'd seen this woman, and if so, who was she.

Barbara had no idea what we were talking about, and she agreed, that she'd seen no such woman in the Gate House.

I related my sighting to Barbara, and the three of us actually walked over to the corner. For some reason, I almost instinctively, reenacted my movements of getting a water bottle out of the barrel, and seeing the woman, '*right there in that corner.*'

Barbara found the entire thing most intriguing, and she was sorry that she'd missed seeing this apparition. Barbara was happy for me, for it was my turn to be the lucky visitor onto the property and to actually see this Victorian lady.

Barbara was all excited and asked me to repeat my story so she could get a video and audio, for the collection of any ghost stories about the properties here. I was happy to oblige and told my story.

I asked Barbara and Jay, if they had heard of any hauntings or legends about the building.

"I've only heard of one story," said Barbara. "I don't know the exact year, but it most likely occurred in the early 1900s. This story has been repeatedly told by water company employees over and over.

"Look up toward the rafters and notice the one that is closest to the upstairs barrister railing.

"The story goes that a distraught employee tossed a rope over, that became a noose. For whatever reason, the man decided to end it all by hanging himself."

Barbara is a believer in ghosts and told me of a ghost experience she had had at the Zorn Avenue location for the Louisville Water Company.

"At the water tower, there stands several buildings, and one such building was an employee only lounge area. By lounge, I mean it had showers and a place to relax a bit.

"The building wasn't the most secure of places, and the door to the shower room had a simple latch with a sliding bar that would read, vacant or occupied.

"After one busy day, I stopped by this building to relax a bit. As soon as I opened the door, I could hear water running, as if someone was taking a shower. All the sounds were as if, someone was in that room, but I knew, that couldn't be possible.

"The exterior door to the building was locked, and I had to unlock the door to enter, so I wasn't expecting anyone to be inside.

"The sliding bar on the door said occupied, but nobody could have gotten inside without the key, and as I stood there, I felt as if something just wasn't quite right.

"I heard the water faucet from the showers turn off, and then, just silence.

"To exit, I had to walk past the door to the shower room, and now, the sliding bar had moved over to vacant, no longer occupied!

"I mustered up the courage and knocked on the door. Of course, there was no response whatsoever, and I reached down and turned to open the door.

"To my surprise, the shower room was wet!

"I didn't waste any time trying to investigate, I just fumbled for my personal things, grabbed my keys and left the building, locking the exterior door," said Barbara.

I thanked Barbara for her time, and I told her, that I'd like to try to come back this evening for the nighttime session.

I returned to the water company that evening and with my dad. He'd never been there and since it had cooled off, he wanted to go. Barbara was still working, but Jay had left and another woman were there. Barbara said she'd been on the lookout all day for the ghost, or anything else strange. I saw nothing else, but apparently, Barbara had mentioned this ghost to a group of Indians from India. She brought over this little boy, about age 9 or so, and his mother, and the young boy asked me about the ghost. So, I told him what I saw.

I can only speculate about the woman. Maybe she was the wife of an employee and was visiting him there, and made an appearance wondering about all the other people there. I don't know, and probably won't ever know. Another theory could be, she was a daughter of one of the male employees and was visiting with him that day. And to throw in a twist of romance, maybe she was engaged to one of the men who worked there and wanted to enjoy some time with her beau.

The "Ghostly" Body Shop on Chestnut

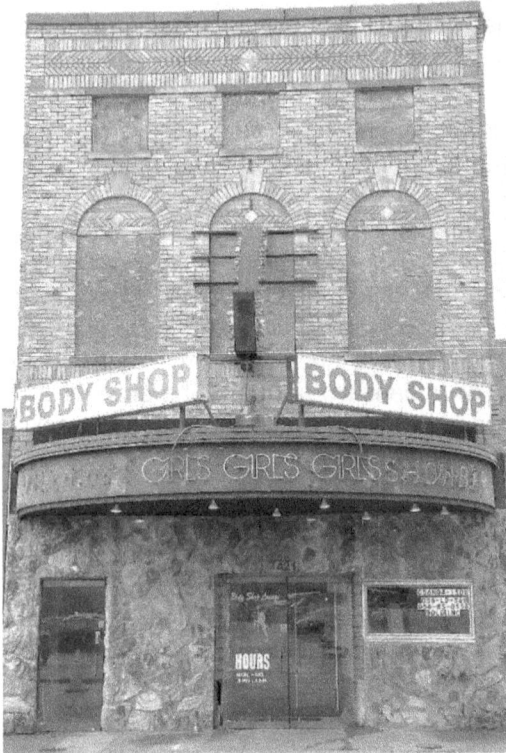

This building has been standing for well over 100 years. Some guests, customers, or ghosts, have decided to stay for all eternity.

It happened just a couple summers ago, when I received a telephone call from a prospective female guest who wanted information about attending a ghost walk. The caller asked all the normal questions, about the cost of admission, locations, and the starting time and duration of the walk. As it so happened on that particular Friday night, I only had the female caller and her companion on the ghost walk. Their names were Candy and Ginger.

The ladies showed up on time and we began the walk. During the course of the walk, I noticed they were interested in the presentation and asked good questions, but still remained preoccupied with time.

"Are you on a time schedule?" I asked, just thinking they had a time commitment and needed to be somewhere else that night.

"We have to be ready for work at 9 PM," was the response from Candy.

Of course, my next question was, "Where do you work?"

"We dance at the Body Shop, over on Chestnut," said Ginger.

Realizing that the ladies were into adult entertainment at the club known as The Body Shop, I couldn't help but smile and chuckle to myself. Knowing this information, I rerouted the tour so we could go to The Body Shop.

"You know that place is haunted," it seemed like both ladies said in unison.

"No," was my surprised response.

"What happened in the building that makes you think it really is haunted?" I asked the women.

By now, we had reached the building and were standing across the street on the south side of Chestnut. It was obvious the building had been standing there for many decades, and from my own personal memory of downtown businesses, it has been several different adult entertainment locations.

Candy pointed to the three windows on the second floor, or windows that once were there, but today, they are blocked and covered. A large, historic neon sign is affixed to the marquee that would shelter the main entrance.

"Those three windows are where our dressing rooms are located. The dancing stage is the center of the building on the first floor, and the bar wraps around the stage, along that one side of the building," began Ginger.

"What is upstairs now? How is that area being used?" I asked the girls.

"See the staircase with the exterior door to the left? That staircase leads upstairs, said Candy. "At one time, a second bar was there, but it isn't used at all since the company doesn't have a second liquor license. So, the second floor is just about deserted; nobody but us, or employees ever venture up there. But, it is an area that we use.

"The first thing that we've noticed that leads us to believe it is haunted is when we'll hear those heavy footsteps coming along the hallway, which is followed by pounding on the dressing room door."

"The pounding has caused me to turn and jump," exclaimed Candy.

"Not many people come up there, so we know that it's not a living person who works there," said Ginger. "We'd call out, 'who is there?'

There would be no answer! One time, we just assumed it was a noise from downstairs, and it pounded on the door a second time, and I thought whoever it was, was going to bust down the door. That really scared me! I slowly walked over and called out, and nobody answered, and I quickly jerked opened the door, and nobody was there."

I just looked at Ginger and thought, '*What in the world is going on here?*"

"On more than on occasion, we'd go downstairs to dance, and we would lock the door, but when we'd go back upstairs, our room had been ransacked! Our dresses would be thrown all over the room, shoes pitched here and there, and even our dresser drawers would be all pulled open and the contents turned upside down and dumped on the floor! Not only did it make us mad, but it also scared us to think, who has been up here and what were they looking for? And we'd go downstairs and ask around, and nobody would have been upstairs, and we left the door locked! Who forced their way into our dressing room and who would trash that room?" said Candy. "I'd have to say that most frightening thing is when that man's face would appear in the mirror!"

"What face are you talking about," I asked.

"This man's face appears in the mirror! We've both seen him," they cried.

"What does he look like? Can you describe him to me?" I asked.

"He's an older looking man, and he's gray! He looks to be from a time period in the past, no resemblance to how people dress or look today! It's his expression that scares me the most, he looks upset and angry, or like he's trying to tell us something," commented Ginger.

"How often does the face appear? Does the man's face just appear, or does it show up when you hear the footsteps, or the pounding on the door?" I asked them.

The women looked at each other, as if waiting for the other to respond first.

"Sometimes, he just appears without any warning, and sometimes, we just hear the footsteps, and sometimes, just our dressing room is ransacked. All of those things upset me! Things don't always come in a sequence," said Candy.

I was invited to drop by and do my own investigation of the business, but I told the girls I would keep in touch. Sometimes, research is just key to piecing together a ghost story and that helps solve the mystery of the ghost.

I was able to keep in touch via email with the two women, and they were able to ask some questions as well.

From my own Louisville research and reviewing of details, I learned that the first "George" Stebbin's Grill opened across the street at 412 West Chestnut Street. There are a few traces of the original building standing today; all you have to do it study the façade of the building. The original restaurant did quite well with steaks and seafood. In the year of 1945, George Stebbins was able to acquire the building that is now known "Body Shop" location at 421 West Chestnut Street. The restaurant was known at that time as the Swizzle, but George Stebbins renamed it as Stebbin's Steak House a little later. The first Stebbin's on the opposite side ceased to exist and just faded away from any recorded history.

The restaurant enjoyed a good run, until the late 1950s when George Stebbin's sold his dining establishment to a gentleman named Leo Weil, who opened the doors as Leo's Twinburger. All of those named restaurants have now slipped away into downtown Louisville restaurant history.

The building at 421 West Chestnut has been standing around for a long time. According to the research and legends of the city, this incident occurred just prior to 1945. The building was a simple dining establishment and sold reasonable priced meals and offered beverages to those looking for something special after the war. The manager's office was on the second floor, and at the time, his office would have had three windows that overlooked Chestnut Street. Today, those three windows are enclosed by the someone else's own design. According to my female dancers from the adult club, those three windows are where their dressing rooms are located.

One night after closing time, the manager was in his office, going over the business receipts and counting the day's profits from the restaurant. According to his account of the events, his office door was locked and secure, when he heard someone running down the hallway. Next, he reported hearing banging on his office door, pounding, almost to the point of busting it down. The manager opened the door, and the assailant charged in with his weapon. Shots were fired, but the manager wasn't killed instantly. The assailant demanded the cash, ransacked the office by searching the desk drawers and dumping the contents onto the carpeted floor. The assailant's actions were quick, and once he got his cash and other valuables, he fled, leaving the manager lying on the floor.

Help soon arrived and the wounded manager was able to give some details of the night's violent attack, but unfortunately, he did not survive the ambush. The assailant was never apprehended.

I do feel as if the dressing room that the dancing girls occupy is haunted. I was able to continue some follow up and made some assumptions of the ghosts. I do feel as if history is simply repeating itself here.

The women, being in the dressing room would hear someone running down the hall, but upon their own investigation, would find nothing. That's the ghost of the assailant making his presence known.

When the women are out of the room performing, the assailant would ransack their room, replaying the events of the night well over 60 years ago, searching for cash or other valuables.

The face that appears in the mirror, is most likely, the face of the manager who met his death in that very room so many years ago.

Is the manager trying to warn the women of impending danger? Is he trying to communicate in some way, trying to protect the women that something like this horrible act, might happen to them?

In the spring of 2016, Cathy Smith and I were standing out front of the Body Shop on Chestnut. I was telling her about the haunting.

As we were starting to walk away to our cars, the door swings open and an older woman, who resembled anybody's grandmother comes out and said, "We're not open until 8:30."

She turned to walk to her car that was parked in front on Chestnut, and I stopped her and said that we were more interested in the hauntings in the building right now.

That sure got her attention. I introduced myself as the owner and tour guide of Louisville Ghost Walks and my companion Cathy Smith.

The woman introduced herself as we shook hands. "My name is Susan, but people around here just call me Evie. I work as the bartender, custodian, whatever needs to be done. I have to do it. I've been here 11 years.

"Have you ever seen or felt like the building was haunted?" I asked Susan.

"Yes," she said without any hesitation. Something is definitely here in this old place.

"What has happened?" I asked her.

"Someone calls out my name, when this place is all closed up and I'm the only one here. Sometimes it is late, so I'll sleep back in one of the parlors; and I'll see shadows, voices, and that is when I think somebody is here in the building, walking around."

Susan invited us inside. It was dark, with only a few Christmas lights strung around the bar. In the corners were some of the flashing disco type dancing lights. As we moved around, we saw the floor of the stage was set upon block glass, with what appeared to be more Christmas light that would illuminate from behind. The stage had a couple of disco lights and several brass colored poles.

The three of us strolled about the bar, and something led me to the large parlor in the back. I parted back the black curtains and looked inside.

"That's where I will sleep sometimes, in that parlor," said Susan.

"Something about that parlor makes even me feel like it is haunted, just something about the room.

"On one occasion, I was bored and sitting up on the stage. I was reading my Bible, when all of a sudden, the black lights just dropped from the ceiling and crashed all around me. I don't know what in the world caused the black lights to just all fall, since none of them are connected together. They just came crashing down! And I spend the rest of the night sweeping up pieces of broken glass."

I asked Susan, "When you are alone in here, and you know the doors are all locked and nobody else is here, and the building is going all crazy with ghostly noises and voices, what do you do?"

Susan looked at me and Cathy and said, as she pointed to the bar and stage area.

"When I hear my name being called, running or stomping footsteps overhead on the second floor, and the building turns real cold, I just get out my Bible and sit on the stage, right next to the pole.

"I will read my Bible, quote scriptures, say a few prayers for the building to calm down, and for whatever restless spirit that is here, to be of peace," said Susan.

"Does it work?" I asked.

"Yes, it does! Once the building calms down and all the strange noises stop, I go back to my parlor and fall back to sleep," she said.

"God does work in mysterious ways," I said to Susan.

We all got a good chuckle out of the comment. I thanked Susan for her time, and Cathy and I exited the building.

Those are questions, that we'll never known the answers to in this lifetime. But the ghost or ghosts still remain, trapped there, for any willing person who happens to occupy the second-floor room of The Body Shop.

The Ghostly Tenants of the Weissinger Gaulbert Apartments

On one of my ghost walks in the late summer of 2017, I was presenting my first story to my group just outside of the Brown Hotel on 4th Street. I noticed a man out of the corner of my eye, just lingering in the distance, listening intently. It's not uncommon for passersby people to stop and listen, so I wasn't alarmed or bothered. What did concern me, was the man approached me as I was speaking and handed me a folded-up piece of paper. I reached out to take the paper, made eye contact with him, and away he went. I didn't stop with my narration to read it. I slipped it into my back pocket.

It's unknown how many tenants have called this building home since construction in 1908. But a few, ghostly residences have decided to stay.

It wasn't until after the walk and I was at home emptying my pockets, that I discovered the paper. I unfolded it, and I noticed it was a take-out menu from a local restaurant. I started to just fold it up and throw it away, but I unfolded it once again, and read his message to me.

The message was written in pencil and in a very precise script. It read, "Have you been in my building to see if it is haunted? The Weissinger Gaulbert Apartment." He included his apartment number and he signed his name. I stopped what I was doing, and just stared down at his message and thought of what kind of hauntings are going on in his building, or his apartment, that he would stop me during the ghost walk to leave me a message.

The next day was Sunday, and his message had stayed with me all morning and into the afternoon. I don't usually investigate private residences because I do respect the privacy and confidentially of the residents, but something was different about his message to me. I was curious and wanted to learn more.

Taking the safe approach and thinking this will be a gamble to make contact with this man, I decided to just write him a letter that contained all my contact information. I thought, worse case, I won't have access to the building, and at least, I can then seal the envelope and deposit it into the nearest mailbox. The post man can deliver it. At least, that is what was racing across my mind. I was too curious to wait for the mail, so I decided to go by in person and look around. Besides, a personal contact is better, at least that's what I've always heard.

I reached the 1908, historic Weissinger Gaulbert Apartment Building at the corner of 3rd and Broadway. It was once a prestigious address for downtown apartment dwellers, and it was rumored to be the first high rise apartment building in Louisville, towering all the way to ten stories.

Upon my arrival, I tried without success at using the security box. All I had to do was enter either the last name or the apartment number. An elderly woman who was in a wheelchair was seated just outside the exterior apartment door. "The box doesn't work; you're wasting your time. That security box hasn't worked in months. Who are your trying to reach?" she asked.

I called the man by name and said I was trying to visit with him in his apartment. She said I'd need the pass code to gain entrance. "I can't give you mine; I don't know you." Then she looked away and said, "Unless you just follow someone inside."

I looked around and four young Asians were headed this way. They accessed the security box with a pass code. I glanced over at the wheelchair bound woman and she gave me a nod and I just followed the four Asians inside.

The elevator was small, but it was large enough for the four Asians and myself. The doors closed and I was then inside the building and riding up.

The elevator stopped at the floor I was looking for, and I stepped off and looked around. Several apartments lined this corridor. Exposed pipes were overhead, and I noticed the carpet looked to be pretty worn. I passed several glossy, white apartment doors that appeared to be heavily scratched and banged up from abuse. I could hear several foreign languages spoken, with these voices coming through the white doors.

I found the man's unit apartment and pressed the doorbell. No response. I knocked. No response. I took a few steps away and assumed he wasn't at home. Then I heard the latch turn. The door swung open.

I introduced myself and then, he remembered me as the 'ghost story guy' from Saturday night. By his facial expression, I think he was surprised that I actually followed up on his message to me.

After some general pleasantries, he joined me in the hallway. He pulled the door slightly behind him, leaving it ajar. "Why do you think your apartment is haunted?" I asked him.

"I hear strange sounds, footsteps, and knocking noises in the apartment, so those things happen. I can't explain them," he said.

He pointed up to his U of L Cardinal cap on his head, "I always wear my cap, and rarely do I take it off, but the cap moves to other places, places where I haven't left it. I find it in places where I know it shouldn't be, or where I know I didn't leave it."

I asked, "Have you ever seen anything, or felt anything, like someone else was with you, or possibly a colder temperature in the apartment?"

He shuffled his feet back and forth, scratched his head and said, "No, nothing like that has happened, but knowing the age of the building, I can't help but wonder if something is haunting the building. I do believe in ghosts.

"Do you know of any hauntings that have occurred in the building?" he asked me.

I told him that actually, he's the second tenant of the building to contact me about a ghost or two in the building.

"I do think something is in your apartment, especially when things get moved about that can't be explained," I told him.

I gave him my contact information and encouraged him to contact me if anything else happened, or if he thought of any other details that might lead to some explanations of what is occurring in his apartment.

He thanked me for my visit and seemed pleased that I took the time to follow up on his note to me. I'm assuming he was pleased that someone was interested in what he had to say about his apartment.

As I mentioned to him, his story was the second one that I'd heard about the building. Since I had slipped into the building, I decided to just roam around a bit to see if I felt anything or was led into a certain area of the building. I felt nothing, so I left.

The first story that I was told, was shared with me a number of years ago. I heard the story, but considering the nature of the topic, I had simply put it onto the back burner until a more appropriate time to share the story.

After my ghost walks, I've made it a habit to walk to 4th Street Live and have some food and beverages at TGIFridays. During ghost walk season, from May to November, every Friday and Saturday night, I'd be at Fridays.

Since I was a regular there, I had gotten to know many of the servers. Two brothers worked at Fridays. One brother was named Charlie, and he was the bartender. I never set at the bar, so I didn't know Charlie too well, but I knew all about him from his younger brother, Tim.

I'd request to sit in Tim's section, and when Tim had slow time, he would join me at the table. That's how I got to know the two brothers. Charlie and Tim lived in the Weissinger Gaulbert Apartment building.

Once the brothers found out I was into the ghost stories and did some investigations, it wasn't too long until the brothers started telling me about ghostly activities that were occurring in their apartment. Sometimes Charlie would stop by and talk with me, but most often, I visited with Tim.

The brothers were in their early twenties. They had a unit that had two bedrooms. They shared it with their mother, so the three called that apartment home. The brothers shared a bedroom, and the mother had the other. From what I understand about the layout, the living room, kitchen, and dining area were in the middle. The two bedrooms were on opposite ends of the unit. The common area that was shared by everyone was in the center. But from what the brothers were telling me, ghostly activity wasn't concentrated in one area; it was all over the apartment.

"I'd come home from work, and walk into the apartment, and I'd notice a strange smell, like something was baking. It was a wonderful smell, but nobody had been at home," said Tim.

"And sometimes," Tim continued, "I'd find some of Charlie's things, like his favorite CDs, his wallet, his new black Converse Chuck Taylor high top shoes, scattered about in the room, and he'd come in and blame me for using or bothering his things.

"One incidence that I recall, Charlie and I almost got into a fight. He accused me of wearing his new black Chucks, because he couldn't find them. I told him I didn't wear them, and I hadn't seen them either. He then accused me of hiding his wallet and helping myself to some money. That really made me angry.

"We argued and I denied this, which only made him madder.

"We both heard this sound, as if someone was walking down the hallway, much like a parent would storm into a room to settle some dispute. It was loud footsteps.

"But nobody was there. When we went to investigate, the hallway was empty, and the apartment door was locked.

"We walked into the living room, and right by the couch, was his black Chucks, and his wallet was on the kitchen table. We'd both been in that room before, and his Chucks and wallet were not there. But now they appeared!

"Now, we've both experienced this. Sometimes, the bathroom would smell all flowery, like powder or perfumes, and we don't use those items," he said with a chuckle.

"One of the strangest of all things, and Charlie has seen this too, was that some of the dishes would be put away from the kitchen. It's a small kitchen, but items would be moved.

"And sometimes, I've noticed that some of the cereal boxes would have been moved away from the top of the refrigerator.

"I had a pair of Levi jeans to just disappear only to be found elsewhere in the apartment. I didn't move them, and they were found folded up and on my bed.

"We've both heard footsteps, as if someone is walking around in our apartment, and this isn't a sound from the hallway. Sure, the building is old, and it does have the usual creaks and sounds, but the steps are from inside of it.

"Doors inside of the apartment have opened on their own, we could be sitting in the living room, and just look down the hallway, and one of the bedrooms doors would just swing open.

"On one occasion, a shadow was seen in the hallway leading toward Mom's bedroom. It moved about, and then just disappeared into the bedroom.

"I've always felt like it was a good feeling, a loving presence, so it never really disturbed me that much.

"Sometimes Charlie would speak of having encounters with our ghost, too, and he'd say that he'd seen the shadow either in the living room or the hallway.

"The strangest thing was, I was sleeping in one morning from a late shift, and I swear, it felt like someone was sitting on the side of the bed. That's what woke me up, feeling the weight of the ghost on the side of the bed.

I'd had conversations with Tim and Charlie over the course of the summer. Sometimes, Tim would just sit with me and almost reminisce about the ghostly encounters, and he'd share them with in a positive way, unlike a feeling of dread or doom that some folks talk about.

I asked him, 'Why do you think it is haunted, or who do you think is haunting the apartment?"

"Oh, I know who the ghost is," Tim said matter of factly.

"You do! Then who is the ghost?" I asked.

"The ghost is my Mom. We soon figured it out, that it was mom's ghost who was haunting the apartment," said Tim.

This was all news to me. Never once did either of the boys mention that their mother was deceased, and it was almost like I felt a huge weight upon my shoulders. I wasn't sure when I wanted this conversation to go to, since Time revealed that the ghost was his mother.

"Mom died; she was a drug addict. Mom overdosed and was taken to University Hospital where she died. She didn't die in the apartment," he said.

"I am so sorry, I didn't know," which was the only words I could say at the time when I heard this news.

"Mom was addicted to prescription pain killers. She'd often buy on the street to handle with her chronic pain, which led to further her addiction," Tim said.

Again, the only words that I could think of saying were simply, "I'm so sorry."

Tim continued, "Mom's ghost is in the apartment. The good thing is, the more that you and I have talked of her ghost, the easier it has been to accept. At first, Charlie and I just thought it was a random ghost, but now, we do think the ghost is our mom, and she's still in the apartment.

"Do you think she's still trying to be your mother all the way from the grave?" I asked.

"Yes, I do. I think she'd doing the things that she used to do when we were growing up, this was way before the addiction happened, and she was a good mother. The prescription pain pills and the addiction took her life.

"I think mom is doing what she would still be doing if she were alive. Doing things around the apartment, maybe cooking something, putting things away, and even coming into the bedroom and sitting on the side of my bed like she did when I was a young boy.

"I do agree with you here, Tim. That explains why you don't feel any fear or sense any danger with the ghost. Have you tried to communicate with her in any way?" I asked.

"No, but sometimes when I come into the apartment, it feels so natural to just call out, 'Mom, I'm home,'" he said.

"I'd say she hears every word you say like that," I replied to him.

My ghost walk season came to a close, so I wasn't at TGIFridays as often. I'd heard that Charlie took a new position elsewhere. I stayed in contact with Tim for a while, and then he left TGIFridays and took a server's position elsewhere. As the winter season passed, I didn't go to 4th Street Live as often, so my contact with both Tim and Charlie faded away. So, when springtime rolled around and ghost walk season resumed, I'd had lost all contact with both brothers.

I still pass the Weissinger Gaulbert apartment building often on my way home, and I still pause and look up at the building from the 3rd Street side. I just wonder, if in one of those units, remains a ghost of a mother, going about motherly duties from the other side of the grave.

The Ghostly Text Message Sent from the Grave

One of the treasures of operating and leading tours with Louisville Ghost Walks, is that I get to meet so many interesting people, and whether people realize it or not, many have at least one interesting story to tell. That's just human nature, I suppose.

At the conclusion of one of my summer walks in 2016, I met a lady and her daughter, who both attended my ghost walking tour.

I can usually tell the level of interest in ghosts when folks linger at the Seelbach Hotel and want to speak with me, and I do encourage guests to talk with me at the conclusion. I mentioned that at the beginning of the walk.

The lady introduced herself as Mary Jane, and her daughter as Sarah. Mary Jane felt compelled to share her story with me, and I found it just as fascinating, and felt like it deserved to be told to my readers.

"My husband, George recently died, back in the spring of 2016. He had been ill for quite some time, so his passing wasn't a shock to me at all.

"Hospice had been called into our home, and I knew that his passing would be a blessing, and not a heartache. It was one of those, 'any day now situations' that I had been expecting.

"George had advanced stages of cancer, and with the illness, he had much difficulty speaking to others and communicating. Very few visitors came by to have conversations with him, yet, people did stop by to just sit by his bedside, and that was comforting to me and to him as well.

"George knew his time was short as well, it was no secret, and all the doctors and medical workers were upfront with us from the beginning.

"When nobody was at home with me and I was in another room of the house, and since George wasn't able to call or speak out my name, he'd use his old flip phone, and just text me a message.

"Our system was working for us, and we relied upon that little procedure to communicate.

"Now, I know, flip phones are just about considered antiques by today's standards, but he wasn't too keen on getting a new one that was higher tech. His old little flip phone worked for me as his message board.

"The day came, and George passed away. He died peacefully, without any big heroic efforts from us or any of the medical staff who was at the house, he just took his last breath and that was it. Upon his death, several of us were in and out of his room, trying to find the right words to say, and to make his body look as comfortable as possible. One of the Hospice workers, noted the time, of 2:39 PM.

"EMS was called to take George away to the hospital, and finally, to the funeral home he'd be transported. EMS made a note that upon their arrival, that George had died, and on their records, we told him, that we recorded his time of death of 2:39 PM.

"It was a afternoon of whirlwind events, but I wasn't hysterical at all, nor was I imagining things. My daughter, Sarah was with me at the house, and I'm grateful for her presence. As George passed by on the gurney, I felt and squeezed his hand one last time, and his body was still warm to the touch! I kissed him good-bye for the last time. Sarah and I stood in the living room of the house, and just held one another as the EMS employees took George out of the house.

"Once we both wiped away and dried our tears, and a took a deep breath, I said to Sarah, 'Let me go get your dad's phone and begin notifying his friends and our family about his death.' I knew his phone had the most updated list of contacts, since when he felt able, he did text with quite a few people.

"I walked into the bedroom, and right by the bedside table, was his flip phone. My cell phone was placed on the charger, right next to his phone. I noticed that my phone was blinking, as if I had a message or something.

"I picked up my phone to read the message, and to my shock, I could see the sender's name, which was George's name and phone number. I clicked on the icon to read his message, and it simply read, '*To Mary Jane, I love you, until we meet again, Love George.*'

'I can't lie here; I almost dropped my cell phone on the floor. In my mind, I could hear his strong, voice saying those words to me- but how could this be?

"Since George's flip phone was next to mine, I reached down and picked up his cell phone. I opened up his flip phone, and in the message window, it read, Welcome AT&T, and I could hear the little chime sound that the phone would make when activated.

"George had a sent message icon blinking, so with my trembling hands, I clicked on the message window to read his 'sent' message. Sure enough, *'To Mary Jane, I love you, until we meet again, Love George'*

"I took a deep breath and called out Sarah's name. Sarah came into the room, and I handed her George's cell phone. I couldn't speak, I just held out the cell phone. She opened it up and read the message. She just stood there, almost stunned, and in a trembling voice, she said, 'Mom, this message was sent at 2:50 PM, after dad's death.'

"Now here is the real twist to this story. I used George's cell phone, and mine as well, to notify our friends and family. For some strange reason, the incoming message from George had vanished from my phone, and on George's phone, there was no record of him sending me a message."

The Heartbroken Girl in Iroquois Park

Iroquois Park, all 733 acres, is a crowning jewel of the southern end of the city of Louisville. It is one of the three famed Olmsted parks the was created in the late 1800s, along with sister parks of Shawnee and Cherokee. Iroquois is a perfect example of old growth forest, situated on rugged knobby hills. Many families, groups, and countless kids and adults alike, enjoy the beauty and charm of Iroquois Park, except one young adolescent girl, named Jessica Thornton.

Very few of my stories involved people that I actually knew, whether on a close and personal nature, or just casually. But Jessica is the exception.

By profession, I've spent close to 30 years teaching middle school. It was during my second year of my career that I was teaching at Southern Middle School, which unfortunately, the building still stands, but the name has been changed.

At that time, I was team teaching and together, we had a total of 60 students to educate. We shared a class of 6th graders and a class of 7th graders. Most of the students weren't the stellar, model students with picture perfect home lives. In reality, many of the students struggled with the daily educational needs, social and emotional needs. Some were simply classified as forgotten students, almost as being unknown to their parents or guardians.

Jessica Thornton joined my sixth-grade class in the winter of that school year. She and her family had moved into the neighborhood, and she had several other siblings. Since I resided in the neighborhood of where I taught, Jessica and some of her siblings started to attend the local church where I was worshiping at the time. During this short time, I was only acquainted with the other siblings, some being younger, and some being older, but never the parents.

In my seventh-grade class, I had a student by the name of Judy House. Judy had an older brother, whom I didn't know, but had heard of from other teachers, and the few conversations that Judy had shared with me about him. I understood that her older brother, Alex House, had several problems in life, and struggled fitting in with society. Alex had a couple run-ins with the law and had a juvenile record that followed him around.

As the winter months passed into the spring, Judy House and Jessica Thornton had become friends. The girls seemed to be a good fit for each other and did spend time together during the day and outside of class.

Spring break finally rolled around, and the students were as excited as they could be. It would be a time for sunshine, pleasant temperatures, and sleepovers at friends' houses, sitting up late at night watching VCR movies and eating pop-corn-all the things that memories for growing adolescences dream of.

I'd heard of the planned sleep-over party that was scheduled for the first weekend of spring break. This event was being held at Judy House's home on Taylor Blvd.

Little did I realize that when I told the students good-bye on that windy Friday afternoon, that would be the last time that I'd say anything to Jessica and Judy.

The Courier-Journal and the local television news broke the story over spring break. People couldn't believe something as twisted and bizarre as this would happen, but it did. It was hard to believe but seeing the pictures on the newscast confirmed the worst.

As detectives pieced together the story and after countless interviews with the young girls that night, and searching the house for evidence, the facts were clear. Jessica Thornton was murdered!

Several girls were staying over at Judy House's home on Taylor Blvd. Typical sleep-over, games, lots of food, movies and conversations about boys. All was going well until an uninvited guest showed up, and that uninvited guest happened to be the tall, dark haired young man by the name of Alex House.

Alex House had paid attention to the young Jessica with some kind words or telling her how cute she looked before this night came to be. To the young Jessica, those were the words she longed to hear.

One thing led to another and Jessica decided to slip off with Alex, just to go for a quick ride in his car. "I'll be right back," Jessica whispered to a friend, "Don't tell anyone I'm gone. Please! It will just be our secret," were her last words as she closed the kitchen door.

Alex and Jessica took off in his car, traveling at a fast rate of speed down Central Avenue, past Churchill Downs, and looping around to Taylor Blvd. The car continued south, until it came to the entrance of Iroquois Park. With one quick right turn, the car was seen speeding up the incline, rounding a curve or two, past the dark golf course, and past the entrance to the walk- up trail to the overlook.

The circle road that goes around the bottom perimeter of Iroquois Park is about four miles in length, of tree lined, secluded curving roads. In daylight, a few scenic vistas are along the way, but in darkness, it transforms into a narrow roller coaster of ups and downs and twists and turns.

Nobody knows for sure if Jessica protested, if she tried to escape, or even screamed. It wouldn't have mattered, because there was nobody there to hear her, see her, or help her.

Alex had pulled the car off to the shoulder of the road and decided to have his way with her, romantically and sexually. Maybe Jessica's attire, or her words or her glances all said 'yes' but deep down, she probably didn't expect this to happen. We'll never know.

When Alex was finished, Jessica was dead. Maybe Alex panicked. Jessica's body was tossed aside and landed up a small hillside. The lifeless Jessica was hidden behind some young, spring growth of plants and trees. Jessica had a colorful bandana tied around her neck, from where she had been strangled to death. Car tracks marked the pavement, as if his car sped off into the darkness, all as if nothing had happened.

Back at the sleep-over, one of the young girls told that Jessica had slipped away with Alex. The time had passed on and it was getting late. The girls became alarmed because Jessica wasn't back yet and neither was Alex. Time moved on very slowly, with more panic in the eyes of the girls. "Where's Jessica and Alex?" were the questions of the night.

"Call the police," said one of the girls. "Tell your parents!" said another. "We can't just sit here, somebody do something!" cried out another. Unfortunately, the girls were home unsupervised, so there was nobody they could call.

Alex returned in the wee hours of the morning. The girls were frantic. Alex had been abusing some drugs by the time he returned to the home. "Where's Jessica?" demanded Judy.

"Where is she?" the other girls cried out.

Alex was in no way able to answer questions. His drug induced stupor left him just about useless.

One of the parents returned to the house from a night out, and the girls spoke up! "Something's happened to Jessica and Alex won't say what! Do something!" chimed another. "Call the police!"

Nothing about this evening is turning out as planned. Jessica's parents were notified, and the police were called. A search began and Alex was questioned.

As the Saturday morning broke daybreak, a search was underway. Alex kept pleading his innocence, and claiming he had no knowledge of Jessica.

But the secret was soon to be uncovered and revealed.

Iroquois Park is the home base of a running club called Iroquois Hill Runners. On Saturday and Sunday morning, many of the running members run or walk the bottom, four-mile loop of the road. Several of the walkers or runners, had rounded that corner and noticed car tire tracks off to the side of the road, which was very unusual. Some large branches were broken down, and it was obvious that a vehicle had been off the road. Someone in the group, walked up the fresh path, and noticed a bandana in the brush. Hidden, down in the brush, lay the body of Jessica Thornton. Dead. And obviously, abused and violated.

The police were called as well as the coroner to this location in Iroquois Park. The mystery was over, Jessica Thornton had been found, but not in the best of way. Jessica's body was removed, family was summoned, tears were shed, and Jessica was soon laid to rest. Or was she?

But the story doesn't end here. Once the facts were printed in the local newspaper, all kinds of people, myself included, drove the bottom ring road of Iroquois Park, pausing long enough to see the crime scene, and to say a silent prayer on Jessica's behalf.

But Jessica's spirit remains there.

"I use the bottom road as a short-cut," began one motorist that agreed to tell me her story.

"I had just rounded the curve and up ahead, I could see a young girl, who was in some form of distress.

"I slowed down the vehicle, and she just darted up onto the hillside, and she just vanished! I had already hit the brakes of my car, and just stopped, and stared upon the hillside where I last saw this girl.

"I couldn't believe my eyes, or what I thought I'd seen, but it was a girl, and I'm sure, it was the ghost of Jessica."

One of the park's maintenance workers had this account to share with me.

"In the spring, one of the responsibilities is to make sure no limbs have fallen from overhead trees. We have to do this after any severe storms as well.

"I knew the area where this horrible crime happened. I was here that week at work, when word broke. I'd been working near the golf course when all the police and media had made the trek to the park.

"Branches had fallen on the road. So, I pulled the truck to the shoulder of the road to remove them. I got out of the truck, and just pulled over the branches to the side, and up the hillside a bit. I looked up, and I realized, I'm now standing in the spot where the girl's body was found!

"I don't think this was my imagination of anything. The morning was warm and sunny, but boy, did the temperature drop as I stood on that spot! I just stood there frozen, and what I heard next was most puzzling. Nobody else was around, no cars, nothing, but I swear, I could what sounded like screams, or cries, and the sounds of someone, not walking, but rushing or running on the ground.

"I'd drive that road all the time, and over the course of that summer, sometimes I'd stop the truck, and walk up the hill side to where it happened. I noticed that summer, that nothing really seemed to grow in that spot on the ground.

"Did her death, even cause the grass in that area to die off as well?" he asked.

A woman named Gayle that I'd spoken with said to me, "One day I was running in the park, and even though I know better, I was running alone. As I approached that area, I saw a girl in the distance, and she was standing in the ditch area, by the black pavement.

"I slowed down my pace to get a better view. Rarely, so I see anyone on this stretch of the road, and never, do I see a child, or a teenager for that matter.

"As I neared her, I did notice that she was wearing a bandana, and the closer I got, she almost faded a bit, and moved upwards, almost disappearing behind the trees.

"I got to the curve and stopped, and even called out, 'Hello, is someone there?' but I got no response. And really, where could she have gone? It was almost like she just vanished.

"I thought it was strange, but I knew I wasn't going to go looking for her. I started back on my run, and as I moved on, I felt compelled to look back over my shoulder.

"I stopped and turned around, and I saw again! The same young figure of a girl standing there, near the pavement and she was in the ditch area. She didn't look my way and I just felt, a real cold chill of air around me. That was odd, because I was hot and sweaty, there was no real for me to feel a chill. But it was real!

"I decided to pick up my pace and run pretty much as fast as I could.

"Then it dawned on me. I remembered hearing the news reports of the young girl who had been brutally murdered back in the spring, and I thought, 'Did I just see her ghost?'

"It had to have been her!"

Motorists, walkers, and bicyclists to this day, report of seeing a young girl off to the side of the road. Jessica's eyes are hollow, and she looks to be in distress, but the people who use this park know better. Sure, she is in distress, and there is a reason for the hollow look in her eyes. All this played out, due to the hands of a substance abusing male, who wanted to have his way with this young girl.

Judy House never returned to the school where I taught.

As of this writing, Alex House remains incarcerated.

Jessica Thornton's ghost still haunts Iroquois Park.

The Mysterious Picture of The Gingerbread House in Savannah, Georgia

Perhaps you've visited and toured Savannah, Georgia. It's one of my favorite places to spend time. I'm thankful that General Andrew Jackson presented the city of Savannah, Georgia to President Abraham Lincoln as a Christmas gift, otherwise it would have burned to the ground.

If you haven't visited Savannah, I'd encourage you to think about it and consider booking a trip there. Enjoy the pedestrian friendly walkways and the parks, the fountains, the architecture that is like no other, the century old houses still standing, and the charm. And I'd be remiss if I didn't mention the ghosts.

Of course, Savannah has ghost stories of pirates, murders and mayhem, crime, and death that you wouldn't be able to escape. Savannah treasures its ghosts, and it does boast that it is one of America's mostly truly haunted cities.

That is a matter of opinion. If not, the city would be a close second to a rival.

On one of my road trips to Savannah in the spring, I was strolling around one of the downtown parks in the historic district.

Street vendors lined the perimeters of many of the parks. Since I'd been to Savannah before, I was familiar with a lot of the architecture of the churches and the houses.

One such house that happened to be in the area of the bed and breakfast that I was staying was The Gingerbread House. Since it was close to my bed and breakfast, I was able to walk past it as my leisure and as many times as I wanted.

I'd never been inside, but it's a property that is easily researched, and is also listed in brochures of walking tours. I was able to read up on the property.

It's been labeled the Cord Asendorf House in honor of the owner. The Gingerbread House, also known as the Asendorf House built in 1899.

Cord Asendorf was married to Bernhardine Asendorf and had four children. He is buried in Savannah's famous Bonaventure Cemetery. The features of The Gingerbread House are unmistakable and stand out as a fully designed home in the Gingerbread style, prevalent in the Black Forest region of Germany. It is framed by a 200-year-old graceful oak tree at its entrance. Inside its doors, visitors will find a conservatory, three fireplaces, a wooden staircase, and extensive wood trim throughout. Antique furnishings from the original period are inside and guests can take a stroll in the private courtyard with a gazebo and small waterfall. The interior of The Gingerbread House also features elaborate architecture of stylish wood trim and a languishing staircase.

Today, the Gingerbread House is used as an event venue; so unfortunately, nobody calls this magnificent structure, 'home' other than ghosts, or spirits, who from some reason, haven't passed on to the next life. It is their home.

Like I'd mentioned, I was enjoying a spring day in the historic district of Savannah. An artist had displayed several of his drawings and artwork against a black wrought iron fence in one of the parks.

As I walked along the sidewalk admiring his work, it was difficult to decide which one that I liked the most. I had several in mind that I wanted to purchase to take home, but that wasn't realistic with my finances and the available wall space at home. I decided upon The Gingerbread House.

His artwork was reasonable in price, almost unbelievable, so I felt like I really made a bargain. I could already visualize this piece hanging in the house.

Some folks who spend a lot of time in paranormal research have commented that ghosts can attach themselves to objects and follow you home. I do agree with that philosophy. Little did I realize; something had attached itself to this piece of art and I was going to be allowing it into my home.

Once I had returned to Louisville, I walked about the house holding up my print of The Gingerbread House, trying to visualize where it would look the best.

I decided the best place for the color scheme used in the artwork, and with the décor of the house, that it would look perfect, centered just above the bed in my bedroom. I wasted no time in having it matted and framed. I was excited and looked forward to the new addition.

Once having it at home, I admired quite a bit. I couldn't help but stop and stare. It looked perfect hanging over my bed, almost as if it had been designed by an interior decorator.

I don't know exactly when things started to happen, such as how many days it had been hanging, or how many nights I'd slept under that picture. But things started to happen that couldn't be explained.

I've never had trouble getting a good night's sleep before. I used to jokingly say that I'd be asleep before my head hit the pillow. Nightmares, bad dreams, restless sleep, sleepwalking, and issues like that have never plagued me. But now, things were about to change.

I'm not sure what happened first, but it wasn't a big dramatic episode. For several nights, I'd wake up, leaning back on my legs, which I'd tucked under my body. My knees would be on the pillow, and my arms would be clasped onto the headboard of the bed. I'd wake myself up, or something would wake me up, and it would be like I had watched some horrible movie or television show, being played within the frame of the picture. All this involved the Gingerbread House!

Scenes would involve fighting! Shouting! People chased one another, both men and women, inside the house, onto the porch, and across the lawn.

After the first or second nightmarish events, I'd wake up, and just stare at the picture in the darkness of the room. I'd reach over and turn on the bedside lamp, and just lean back resting upon my tucked-up legs, and just stare at the picture. Even though the room was dark for sleeping, certain aspect the house stood out, almost like a light was shining in the various rooms.

One night I recall walking up, and I was reaching up, and touching the glass of the picture, as if something was to be felt.

Being a rational adult, I'd tell myself that it was something I'd eaten prior to retiring, or stress, or my mind just couldn't relax and allow me to have a good night's rest. But I was only fooling myself.

On another night, I woke myself up, holding onto the frame of the picture! In the dream for that night, I was inside the house, or just standing in the doorway of the front door. I saw male and female characters who were running in fright from something that was chasing them. I don't recall who was doing the chasing, maybe that perpetrator's character never made an appearance, but the male and female characters were running in fear from something, human or ghostly, remains to be known. The characters were running throughout the rooms in the house. Down a main staircase, into a dining room, past a bedroom, and down a hallway. As the dream continued, I had moved from the doorway of the house. In the dream, I was standing sidewalk, and they came busting out of the house, toward me. At that point, I woke up, holding onto the frame, and my heart was racing. I can't say for sure, if I was trying to remove the print from the wall, or if I was just holding onto the frame.

A few more days passed without anything happening. I got to the point that I was feeling anxious prior to my going to sleep. I'd gotten over that feeling of excitement of wondering what might show up in my dreams that involve the picture of The Gingerbread House, and now, I was trying to go to sleep with a feeling of dread, of, 'what might happen next?'

When I'd have a dream, it would leave such an impression on me that I'd think about what I saw in the dream during the course of the day. I'd try to piece something together, trying to see if the dreams were in any sequence or if characters from another night, would show up in another nightmarish dream. I don't recall any characters making repeat appearances. From the best of my memory, the characters were all new.

The nightmarish dreams concerning The Gingerbread House continued. The dreams wouldn't occur every night, and sometimes, it might be a week or more between them. But, sometimes, I'd have a nightmarish dream in sequence of the nights.

I was always hesitant to tell people about these dreams. In some ways, I was afraid they would think that I was showing signs of some form of anxiety or hallucinations or something.

On another night one of the nightmarish dreams was more intense than the previous ones. It involved a murder. In the main hallway of the house, three men were grouped. Words were exchanged and shouting was heard. One of the men was wearing what looked like a tuxedo, and the other men were in regular street clothes. In the dream, I heard a loud bang, representing the pistol being fired by the man in the tuxedo. I woke myself up, again on my knees, holding the edges of the picture frame, crying out, "No, you shot him!"

My heart was pounding! I was able to gain my breath and after a few minutes of just sitting up on my knees in the bed, I laid back down. I wasn't ready to go back to sleep. The dream was vivid, more violent, and came with a loud, gunshot bang.

Several days now passed without any of the nightmarish dreams. I kept wondering, am I seeing events that at one time occurred in the house? Is this print of The Gingerbread House, now a portal to the dark and sinister events that changed people's lives forever?

One night in a dream, I witnessed a violent attack on a woman. This scene played out in the upstairs bedroom. I wasn't able to see the attacker, but I saw the entity move upon the woman, who had struck the woman. This time, I was a character in the house. I was in the room, and the room was out of any proportion. As I tried to run to help the woman fend off the attacker, the room's rectangle shape just increased as I ran toward her. When I woke with a jolt, I had removed the framed print from the wall and I was holding it against my chest. I'd never removed it from the wall during the dream sequences, but this time, it was different. I had removed it. I'm still amazed by the fact that I had the frame print and no damage was done to it.

By this time, I'd started taking a mild, over-the-counter sleeping medicine so I could sleep and not have these nighttime visions. The dreams were becoming intense, especially if I'm in The Gingerbread House either as an active character or just a spectator.

On another occasion in one of the dreams, I was outside on the sidewalk facing the house. I heard a scream, and I went running up the sidewalk and bounded upon the porch. The sidewalk seemed to get longer as I ran, but eventually, I made it to the front porch. I pushed open the front door and charged up the staircase. As I ascended the staircase, it never ended. I kept going up, trying to reach the second floor, but that didn't happen. I kept following the scream, but found no source, because the staircase never ended.

When I woke up that morning, I couldn't believe my eyes. I had removed the framed print from the wall, and I had propped it up against the table that was parallel with the bed. As I sat up on the bedside that morning, I looked down at the print, and turned and looked up at the blank wall over the bed, where the printed frame had hung, hours earlier.

When did I actually removed it from the wall? That remains a mystery.

Looking at my log of events that I'd started taking, I'd noticed the intensity of the dreams increased, plus sounds effects were added, and I'm no longer a spectator, but an actual character in the dream who is inside of the house. I'm playing a role in The Gingerbread House, a house that I'd never set foot inside.

I'd started talking to people about the nightmarish dreams. Some would look at me in disbelief. Some would offer advice; some would say that I need to remove the print from my house. Some suggested that I try to contact the artist, and some suggested that I contact the owners of The Gingerbread House. Some of the suggestions made sense and were reasonable. I had no way to contact the artist at that point, and even in that time, it would have been a challenge to contact the owners of The Gingerbread House. Besides, in my mind I'd rehearsed what I would have said to whomever answered the phone.

How do you explain to someone over the phone, and ask about murders, assaults, screams, and staircases that never end, to a property owner, and you confess that you'd never set foot inside the house? And how do you explain that all this started happening when I purchased a print from a street artist?

This print was causing me too much worry and anxiety. But, on the other hand, I wasn't quite ready to have it removed. In one regard, it was almost like, what's going to happen next in the house? It was almost like a series on television and I never knew what would play out.

Prior to my saying that 'enough was enough' I'd had one more troubling dream. This one involved soldiers, possibly from the Civil War, however, Savannah didn't really see much battle of the Civil War. Maybe restless spirits from battles in Georgia had made their way to the house, but again, that remains a mystery. I recall bodies in the house, some covered with white sheets, and others wounded, with very crude bandages. Many of these soldiers, or characters, just moved about the house from one room to another. Some stared at me, probably wondering who I was and why I was dressed the way that I was dressed, if it was a Civil War dream.

When I woke that morning from having that dream, the print of The Gingerbread House wasn't hanging over my bed. It wasn't positioned against the table that was parallel with my bed. I got out the bed and scanned my eyes around the room looking for the print.

This time it was leaning up against the foot board of the bed. I stood there looking down at the print. During the night, I'd gotten up, removed it from the wall, left my bed and at this point, slept-walked and placed it against the foot board.

So, at this point, I realized that I'm not just taking it down from the wall and leaning it against a nearby table, but I'm actually sleep walking and standing the print up in a new location. I had absolutely no memory of doing any of this.

It was suggested that I be more proactive and that being, at bedtime, to just remove it from the wall and place it behind my headboard and lean it against the wall. That advice sounded reasonable to me for I followed it.

Nothing happened for the upcoming nights, no nightmares, no sleepwalking, nothing. For what seemed like weeks now of tormenting dreams that all involved The Gingerbread House, they had ceased. I never really knew the source or what had happened in that house to have played out in such a vivid way in my subconscious. But the characters all came to life within the frame.

The Gingerbread House print remained behind my headboard for several weeks, and it never returned to the position held over my bed. I never hung another picture or artwork over my bed, that location remained blank.

When the time came for me to move and I was able to purchase my own house, I knew upfront that The Gingerbread House would not be positioned in my new bedroom. In fact, I was a little unsure it I wanted to take it with me. I'd heard stories of ghosts attaching themselves to objects, and if that was true to me, I didn't want it to rob me of my sleep and take possession of my dreams.

Time passed. Once I got settled into my new place, I removed The Gingerbread House print from the back room where I had it stored. I carefully tore back all the brown newsprint and masking tape that it had been wrapped up in. The print was in perfect condition and still, looked just as intriguing to me as the day that I purchased it from the street artist. I wanted to keep it and display it in the house.

I really did like the print with all the details, the color scheme, and just the look of the house itself. I found a new location in my house and today, it's hanging in my piano room, a room that I have no intentions of ever, trying to go sleep in.

I've never had another nightmare that involved The Gingerbread House to this day Unfortunately, I've never returned to Savannah, but when I do, I plan on visiting The Gingerbread House.

Union Station is a jewel to the city of Louisville. The building is rich in history, romance, heartache, and ghost stories.

Union Station, Traveling Ghosts Downtown Louisville

From construction in the early 1880s and continuing until 1976, Union Station at 10th and Broadway played a very important role in the history of public transportation in the city. The first train rolled into the station at 7:30 A.M. on September 7, 1891. Union Station reached it all-time peak in 1922, with a total of 120 trains arriving and departing daily.

By the mid-1970s, only 76 trains entered and departed Union Station. The final "All Aboard" was called on October 31, 1976, when the last passenger train left Union Station for Nashville. Today, the building is the main office of TARC (Transit Authority of River City) bus transportation center for the city. TARC took possession of the building in 1979.

TARC valued the building and spent a fortune with restoration of the building. The building has thick, masonry walls, large, operable windows, ceramic tile and pine wood floors, red oak wainscots, marble and raised paneled walls, stain glass skylight and rose windows. A rose window, twenty-four feet in diameter, dominated each end of the atrium. Looking upwards, the atrium features a large vaulted ceiling lighted by a skylight of 84 panels of stained glass. Several art glass panels grace both the north and south facades. Several of the original benches remain in place today in the lobby. The architecture design for the exterior was completed with a massive façade, Seth Thomas clock tower, turrets, and smaller towers all incorporated into the design. The main atrium, or concourse, had a dining and women's retiring rooms, and ticket counters. The mezzanine contained the railroad offices.

Scores of individuals passed through the Broadway entrance and exited out onto the train shed to board their train to distance destinations, while others, entered the building from the train shed and into the grand lobby of the building. Some travelers may have the fondest of memories inside the stately building called Union Station, arms embraced with joyful hugs and kisses, while others, may still carry painful, memories of their sad departures of loved ones going off to war- and unfortunately never returning.

When you consider demographics of the city, just about every immigrant to Louisville entered the city through the doors of Union Station. Three United States Presidents, Franklin D. Roosevelt, Harry S. Truman, and Dwight Eisenhower also arrived in Louisville through Union Station.

I was able to make several visits to Union Station, and I had permission from the TARC administrators to interview employees and to tour the building. The employees that I spoke with were long term employees who love the building and enjoy working in such a grand and stately building.

When the accountant Jane heard that a gentleman was here doing research on ghostly activity within the building, she was excited to have the opportunity to speak with me.

"I feel a lot of love in this building. When I look into the lobby or walk the silent hallways or corner stairwells, if I sense ghosts, the energy isn't negative at all.

"This is the presence that I I feel this a building," explained Jane. "It is a building with a lot of love, many hellos were said here, and tearful goodbyes."

Carl was another worker for TARC that agreed to speak with me. Another employee, named Samuel was with us, and Jane, from upstairs in accounting came along, too.

Carl said, "I work in building maintenance, and I've been here for years.

"This is probably one of the few buildings in downtown Louisville that has ghosts, and not ghosts from people, but ghosts from animals!"

"What are you talking about, ghost animals?" I asked Carl.

"Ghost cats," Carl said with a smile.

"Let's go down to the basement, and I can show you what I'm talking about; and we even have the remains of the great fire of 1905. The beams and floor joists still have evidence of the fire, even with scorched marks!"

We descended the staircase and walked along a narrow passageway. It was lined with brick archways creating a cavernous maze of twists and turns. Hoses were sprawled about the concrete flooring. In a couple locations, we had to use wooden footbridges over ditched areas that had been dug out in the floor and filled in with gravel. As we walked past the north end of the building, we could hear the rumble of traffic on Broadway. Stepping along the dark floor and turning to walk south, on the western side of the building, water had puddled on the floor and the occasion drip, drip, drip was heard overhead. Only a scattering of bare light bulbs hung from the rafters and charred floor joists that supported the lobby were overhead.

Our guide Carl reminded us to be very quiet as we walked to the area, so not to disturb the ghost cat and hopefully, to be able to hear it for ourselves.

"I've always heard of the ghost cat, but really, this basement scares me and I wouldn't be down here alone anyway," commented Jane in a hushed tone to me. "The last thing I'd want to see if a ghost cat!"

We reached an area of the basement and some cracks of the exterior daylight shown through the upper beams and storage doors on the western side.

We stood in silence just waiting for something to happen. Noises echoed in the spacious basement. There was a clang from a pipe overhead, followed by quietness of or own breathing. A hiss from a boiler broke the silence, next came the swoosh of air circulating, and a knock from some distance area were all heard.

My eyes got used to the darkness. A jagged ray of outdoor light cast its glow on the floor. Scanning around, nothing but multiple shades of blackness could my eyes see.

The four of us just stood there, waiting patiently for something, a sound, anything to confirm that presence of a ghost cat.

"Meow!" A little softer a second time, "Meow!"

"Shhh," went Carl with his finger to his lips. He whispered, "It's here."

I looked around the room and at the others who were with me. We stood there in disbelief, questioning whether what we were hearing was actually the famed 'ghost cat' that haunts the basement.

There it went again, 'meow,' creating a sound that seemed to be coming from a few feet of where we were standing, but not a cat was in sight at all.

Jane's mouth dropped open, and we looked at each other.

Nobody made a sound at that point, and unfortunately, neither did the ghost cat. At least three audible meow sounds made by the ghost cat was sufficient evidence.

"Where did it go? Where is it?" I asked and the others, questioned that same thing.

Carl pulled out his industrial flashlight and cast a light over to the side where we hear the meow sounds, and nothing was in the way to obscure our view. No columns, no building structures holding up the massive building above us, no hoses on the floor, and no gravel dug out ditches. All we could see was the open space. There was no place for a cat to hide.

Carl pointed his flashlight up toward the floor joists above us and we could clearly see the scarred beams from the fire.

"According to the history, the fire was in November of 1905.

"A mother cat gave birth before the fire, so she had her kittens downstairs in this lower level. This was the location that horrible night. The fire raged, and with any fire, fragments of the building and ceiling were falling down. The mother cat apparently sensed danger, and she moved each kitten to a higher location from where they normally stayed.

"The fire didn't get them; the water did. At least six feet of water was in this basement. The kittens drowned in what was considered by the mother cat to be a safe, higher location. However, the mother cat didn't drown, nor did she die in the fire.

"One kitten survived, a male, with the markings of a Maltese Cat. The kitten was finally rescued from living as a stray kitten out in the building. The kitten was caught by Capt. Roberts, who was the station master. Capt. Roberts perceived the kitten to be wild, mostly from the trauma he experienced as a young cat. Capt. Roberts named the kitten, "Tom-cat" and he became the station pet. Tom-cat was treated as a pet.

"One afternoon the mother cat was found dead. Her head had been severed and her lifeless body was found out by the train shed by the tracks.

"Workers who tend to work down here in this area, often speak of the sounds of cats, or kittens in certain areas of the basement. A lot of the guys will stop what they are doing and just go investigate because the noises of meows and cat calls sound so real, some guys have to search it out.

"Other guys have mentioned that they have seen a cat or two, way off in the distance down here. Of course, the cat always looks real and it's a mystery as to how a cat would be down here, but again, the guys would go searching or trying to follow the cat and find out how it gets into the building.

"Guys like myself who have been here for a long time, just tell them, you can go searching all you want, but it's a ghost cat and it won't be found. You can follow the sounds all over the basement, but you won't see or find the cat.

"I don't know if it is the ghost of Tom-cat, or the mother cat. Nobody has mentioned anything about a headless cat down there, and frankly, I don't want to see a headless cat here either," stated Carl.

Samuel, another maintenance worker, was walking with us on the tour. He spent a lot of time in the basement as well with this job responsibilities.

We left this side of the building and journeyed over to the eastern side. On the eastern side of the building is one of the remaining Station Master Offices.

"I was a new employee here, and now, I've been here about 15 years," began Samuel "I had just come down here from the main staircase over there and rounded this corner. Some men were working here on some of the HVAC systems that ran from the original building, L & N at 9th and Broadway, and we're in this location at 10th and Broadway. Piping systems run from that building, through a tunnel system, over to this building. The two buildings shared heat. Plus, the tunnel allowed administration employees a way to walk between the two buildings and not be outdoors in the weather.

"I had just stood up and had my tools in my hand. I turned around and just reached up to wipe my brow. I sighed and looked over to where something had caught my eye.

"At first glance, I thought it was just another one of the railroad workers, but this guy was in full uniform. He was standing there, just until he disappeared! People just don't disappear like that."

"What was he doing?" I asked.

Samuel responded, "He wasn't doing anything. He was just standing there by the door to his office.

"He was in the navy-blue uniform with the brass buttons and hat. He had a thick mustache, too. The way he was standing, he could have just walked out of the Station Master office and he was just scrutinizing the work that was being completed. His eyes were focused toward the tunnel and the HVAC workers.

"Within seconds he was gone! I stopped and spun around, looking over my shoulder thinking to myself that people just don't disappear like that.

"I asked the other guys who were working HVAC, 'Did you see that guy?'

"Those men stopped and commented back to me that they didn't see anyone and asked what I was talking about. I stood there and described him to the guys.

"Those guys just gave me blank stares, one scratched his head, and another stooped back down and went back to his work. Another chuckled to himself and shook his head in disbelief of what I said."

I asked Samuel to show me this area. We took a few steps away from the sealed-up tunnel's passageway. I looked at the door, and to this day in brass letters, the words "Station Master" is still visible on the door.

"How is this area used today? Or, what did the station master use this room for?" I asked.

"Today, we just use it as a storage room, but for the station master, it would have been his office; and it could have been used as a sleeping room, too. It was private, plus he would do his work, keep important papers secure, or sleep if he had been here for a long time."

"People just don't disappear like that," exclaimed a worker who had seen a ghost at this location one day.

Samuel opened up the Station Master's door and I stepped inside. Various items were being stored in there. I noticed that it had a brick, vaulted ceiling and shelving units that was full of old, yellowed papers. Time had stood still in this room.

I assumed that TARC probably doesn't use this room for anything today.

Carl and Samuel escorted me through a shortcut to the back side of the building.

"During wartime, this was the makeshift morgue," began Paul, another one of the employees that joined us by the Station Master's office on our building tour.

"Caskets were brought in here via the tunnels; the train station didn't want the caskets lined up in the lobby. The baggage shed was just above us, and the ramp would have been used to wheel in the caskets as they were removed from the baggage cars of the trains.

"Some of the deceased soldiers in the caskets had to play the waiting game. Some of the soldiers had to wait to be claimed by family members. Picture one casket after another, lined up here. Spouses, or parents, had to come down here to view the body to make sure it was the right person. You know, records sometimes got lost or mixed up. Some of the deceased soldiers had no identification or were too damaged.

"Of course, it would be very emotional for the loved ones; the family or the spouses had to identify the body, but it had to be done.

"At that point, the body would be loaded onto a departing train or sent elsewhere in the state, or across the country to waiting family members for burial.

"A lot of the guys, and even the ladies who work upstairs, have to come down here for office supplies or whatever they need.

"You always hear talk of hearing distant moaning and crying, and footsteps. People stop and look around, and nobody is there.

"A couple of the women who work in marketing for TARC, have to come down here, and some of them just won't do it.

"This one lady named Karen, has told me over and over again, that she always brings a buddy with her down here. Karen says that she feels like someone is watching here or following her down here. Karen says, she gets the sensation that she's not alone at all down there," said Paul.

I do agree, it is dimly lit, and a lot of building construction and supports block a lot of the viewpoints. I can understand why she'd feel that way. Plus, just the knowledge that this area at one time was lined up with caskets of soldiers from WWII. I can just picture it as well.

The guys led me back up to the main lobby of Union Station.

Debbie, another long-term employee, was waiting for me. Her office is located on the eastern side of the mezzanine.

"I got to the point where I was hearing all kinds of ghostly noises, but I never really got used to them. I got to the point of expecting sounds, not natural sounds that would be heard here, but strange noises."

"What do you mean, strange noises?" I inquired.

"The loudest was a bowling sound, and it would just be in the room that I would be in. I've mentioned to other people, and they'd never hear anything. I've mentioned it to the HVAC folks, and nobody could identify it at all. It would just be a crash sound, almost like I was in a bowling alley.

"I'd hear noises like someone was coming into the room behind me, and I'd stop, turn around and even say hello, and I'd be speaking to an empty room or a closed door.

"Geoff's office is just across the mezzanine on the west side of the building. Geoff has been in agreement with me. He speaks of hearing footsteps coming down the hallway, but nobody is there. He'd stop and go look, and mention about hearing footsteps against the tiled floor, heavy footsteps, as if a man is walking.

"I don't really feel scared, but in the evenings I'm ready to go. I don't want to be up here alone. I like knowing that other employees are close by, but just that feeling that I'm not alone, something ghostly is here bothers me.

"Maybe it's a past railroad employee that's still hanging around the building. Passengers wouldn't have been up here that I know of.

"There's way too many offices, stairwells, and doors for something to be lingering around. Some days I just don't like that sensation that something else is here, especially on days when it really is 'noisy.'

In the lobby, I was able to meet Leonard. Leonard has been a part of the afternoon custodial staff for at least ten years. While talking about ghosts, he'd smile a bit, stare down at the floor, and act kind of nervous.

"Everything changes around here when the upstairs employees leave at the end of the day. Boy, does this place seem big, bigger than what it is during the day.

"It's one thing to wave and tell folks goodnight and know, they have turned out their lights and locked their office door. By the time I arrive there on their floor, the door would be unlocked, cracked open, and the office lights turned on.

"From standing down here in the lobby, it's pretty easy to look upwards to the mezzanine and it will be dark, and a few minutes later, the lights will be on. I'd walk up there and turn out the lights, and by the time I'd get back downstairs and resume what I was doing, the lights would be turned on.

"I'd be working down here, and I'd clean the restrooms, both men's and women's rooms. I'd know for a fact; I'd leave the restrooms clean and the doors would be closed. Next thing I'd know, the restrooms doors would be open.

"At night when it's quiet in here, I'd hear the footsteps of someone walking above on the mezzanine. I'd put the broom down and move out here and look up. I'd hear the steps and follow them with my eyes, and there would be nobody there.

"One night, I was determined to go see what the going on upstairs. I kept hearing sounds, like someone walking.

"I walked up the steps and, as I neared the top, I could hear more of the shuffling of the feet. My heart started racing a bit, because I was just around the corner and I could hear the steps.

"I paused and what I noticed on the flooring was a shadow. It was the shadow of someone who was standing, and that individual was just around the corner.

"I thought to myself that whoever it is, is just right there. I took a deep breath and called out, 'Custodian here, who's up here?' but I didn't get a response.

"I took another deep breath and moved closer, and the shadow of a man that was cast on the floor, just faded from sight.

"I rounded the corner, still expecting to see someone standing there. I was hoping it was an employee playing a trick on me, but as I whipped around, nobody was there.

"I moved over the edge of the railing on the mezzanine and looked down, and the other custodian was down in the lobby with his pushcart of supplies.

"I called out to him, 'Have you seen anyone up here, or heard anyone walking around?' and he said, 'No, not a soul.'

"Standing there, I looked up and down the walkway, never heard anything or nor seen anyone. I did walk on down the western side of the mezzanine and checked all the doorknobs.

"The other custodians down in the lobby, shouted up to me, and asked what I was looking for. I just told him that I heard footsteps and thought someone was up here. I was just checking it out.

"See, that wasn't the only episode that I've experienced in here.

"Once, I was over by the staircase on the west side, and I was going downstairs, and I felt on the landing, this brush of cold air, as if someone passed me going up. The sensation was followed by the sounds of footsteps on the steps.

"I knew nobody was there, just the sounds of some long-ago passenger or employee going somewhere in the building.

"Trains had left this place a long time ago, but someone still has business in the building."

Leonard picked up his broom and said with a smile, "All I can say is to the ghostly passengers, 'please don't miss that train! I don't want you hanging around here with me, forever.'"

Author's Note: In the story, I referenced some men working on the HVAC system and the piping in the tunnel. This HVAC system provided heat from the main office at 9th and Broadway to the Union Station terminal at 10th and Broadway. As I was researching, interviewing, and gathering the details to complete this story, I found out that my own father, who was an L & N Railroad employee for 44 years, was one of the guys assigned to work on the HVAC system and that he was there that day when the sighting occurred of the station master.

Wagner's, A South Louisville Tradition with a Ghost

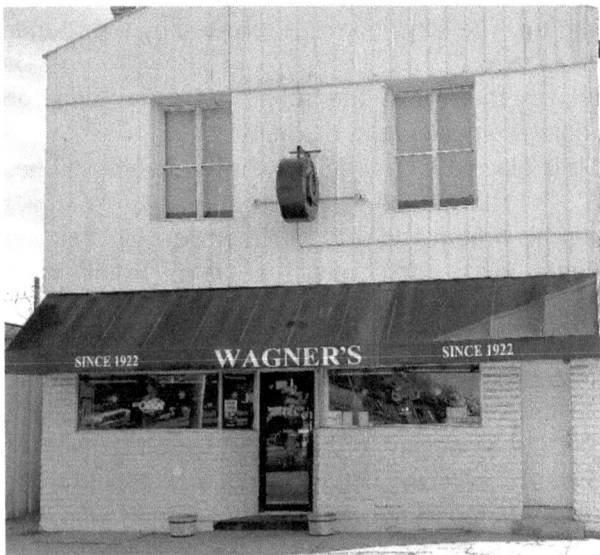

Wagner's has always been a mainstay for Churchill Downs and for hungry patrons at the corner of 4th and Central Avenue.

Leo Wagner opened up Wagner's Pharmacy in the year of 1922, when he purchased Hagen's Pharmacy. The pharmacy occupied the northeast corner of 4th Street and Central Avenue for decades, until the city announced plans that Central Avenue was going to be widened for accommodate changes in the neighborhood, and for Churchill Downs.

Wagner's built a solid reputation of providing pharmaceutical medicines to the men who worked at Churchill Downs. Mr. Wagner was a friend to those folks who labored so hard in the horse racing industry. He never turned down a man in need, often doing business on credit to support those employees who were short on cash.

Mr. Wagner also became a mainstay in the community with products for horses, so he was almost a local veterinary. Even to this day, the Wagner's name is attached to products for horses.

At that time period in early American history, most pharmacies had a soda fountain, or a counter that served up short order foods.

As time passed in the community, Wagner's was known for an outstanding, hearty breakfast, and fried fish sandwiches. Nobody ever left Wagner's hungry, unless by choice.

In 1989, word came that Wagner's was moving, not far, just across Central Avenue on the southeast side, to the former Tom and Edna's Café. Wagner's wanted to remain in the neighborhood, besides, it was now an institution and couldn't depart from its roots.

As Tom and Edna's Café emptied out, as much of the original pieces of furniture from the original Wagner's made the trek across the street. Tom and Edna's steam table went out one door, and the original counter and 12 stools were moved inside. The ice cream chest, and the beverage dispenser was there. Tables from the booths were positioned. Countless photographs from Derby horse races now covered the walls. White oval plagues hanging just about the grill on the wall, all hand painted, showed the menu choices of delicious food once served up by the short order cooks. The plagues menu ran the gambit of hamburgers, soda, cherry pie, a cup of coffee, and of course, breakfast.

Now, the furnishings weren't the only things that traveled the short distance. Some still believe the ghost of the senior Mr. Wagner made the journey as well!

Mr. Wagner,Sr., opened the original Wagner's Pharmacy. He had a son, and his name was Lee Wagner. The second Lee Wagner fathered four children, and his son is also named, Lee Wagner. The second Lee Wagner passed in the year of 2008. The third, Lee Wagner, manages the restaurant today.

During the summer of 2017, I had the opportunity to meet Lee Wagner after having a meal there. I expressed my interest in the restaurant and brought up the topic of any ghostly activity. He smiled a little as he thought about my inquiry. He said he wasn't aware of anything ghostly, but he also didn't deny the possibility of the restaurant being haunted. Lee hadn't given it any thought of his granddad or even father coming back to the place they both loved so much. But I know I gave Lee something to think about! He gave me his blessing to ask him employees to see what they had to say on the topic.

On a follow up visit one morning for breakfast, my server that time was Cheryl. When the breakfast rush had calmed a bit, I thought this would be a good time to start some dialogue.

"Have you ever experienced anything ghostly here in the restaurant?" I asked her.

Cheryl paused and looked at me in some disbelief as to what I was asking. "As a matter of fact, yes, I have."

"What happened to you? How long have you worked here?" I asked.

"I've only been here a few months; I started prior to Derby. One of my job responsibilities is to make sure all the tables have the sugar caddies well stocked after each shift.

"I can stuff those caddies and turn around, and some of the packets of either sugar or sweetener is missing, and I know I had the caddy crammed full.

"One day, I was finishing up from lunch and the restaurant was closed. I came in the next morning, and someone asked me, 'Why did you leave the sugar packets all scattered about on the tables?'

"I looked around that morning, and sure enough, some of the sugar packets and sweeteners were still scattered about on tables. I said I didn't leave them that way; all the caddies were stuffed full."

A few minutes later, I was able to make contact with Martha. Martha has worked there for several years, so she should be a good resource. I asked her the same question, "Do you feel like the restaurant is haunted?"

"I've been here for years," she began.

"The only ghosts that I'm aware of, are the ghosts of the original owners, Tom and Edna."

"Why do you think it's the ghosts of Tom and Edna?" I asked. I wasn't expecting that answer.

"I've been here real early, and I'd hear what would sound like chairs moving about or scooting across the floor.

"Tom and Edna used to live upstairs, and we don't use the upstairs at all."

"There's no reason for those sounds to be heard overhead!" I commented back.

"Have you experienced anything else, or given any thought as to why they are haunting the building?" I asked.

"Tom and Edna's were at the location for years, and I think they haven't left. Their presence is still trying to manage this business. They had a large steam table here, and their spirits are still in the restaurant.

"Here's the conflict, if this is true.

"When Wagner's moved over here, they brought over the counter and the stools and moved out the steam table.

"This is the original soda fountain, hood over the stove, and even the signage for some of the food items that was served when Wagner's was across the street.

"Sometimes I wonder, if the ghosts of Tom and Edna are a little confused about what is going on here?"

A few minutes later, I was able to speak with Pam, another one of the servers at Wagner's.

"I've seen the ghost of Mr. Wagner, the senior guy! One morning, I was walking to the back of the building, where the pharmacy used to be.

"Today, it's no longer a pharmacy at all. But we've got all kinds of medical supplies that the horsemen from Churchill Downs would need.

"I looked up, and there stood Mr. Wagner! He was just standing at the pharmacy window, looking inside as if he were looking for some medicine or something to give to a customer.

"He was actually gray in appearance! I saw him in full body, and he lasted just a few seconds, and then he faded from sight. He was gone.

"There was no doubt in my mind who that was, and that was his ghost."

Another server that I was able to speak to was named Claire. She had only one ghostly activity in the building. In the kitchen area where most of the food is prepared for the diners, the doorway that leads to the upstairs was propped open.

Claire reported that something had to have removed the door stop, and the door closed on its own. Something had to have reached down and either kicked the stop, or moved it with their hand, for the door to close. The door isn't going to close on its own without some help.

The last employee that I was able to interview was named Marlene. "I started working here shortly after I retired from my other job, and that was in 2010. I needed something to do, and I liked that I'm right here in the neighborhood. This is a good place to be, and the ghost doesn't bother me.

"I don't wait the tables but tend to work more in the office and in the back where the pharmacy used to be.

"I tend to sell more liniments and medicines for the care of the horses and the horse trainers that might need something.

"I was working in the back and I heard the glass doors open, as if someone came inside.

"Nobody was there, but I could feel the cool air from when the door was opened, and it closed.

"I just said, 'Come on in, Mr. Wagner!'

"And I think he did... and he's still here," said Marlene.

"The house is alive. The house picks and chooses who volunteers here, who visits, who walks up the steps of the property. Even before people know it, the house decides what happens here," stated Gwen, a volunteer who maintains the house.

The Whispering Voices at Whisper's Estate

Mitchell, Indiana

I'd became acquainted with Whisper's Estate when I watched a local newscast on haunted properties in the area. Mitchell, Indiana, is about 70 miles northwest of the city of Louisville, and the local newscast provides news for that area.

The house didn't look 'that haunted' in the newscast as the reporter led the way through the haunted house. In fact, I thought it was a residence, but the new owner only stayed in the house for four nights, until he was chased out! Not by the living, but by the dead!

I was able to contact the owner, Mr. Vance, and he was able to connect me with two ladies, Gwen and Sonja, who maintain the house. These two ladies also lead tours for guests who want to investigate the house.

Mr. Vance purchased the house in 2008. Both ladies joined the house's staff in 2010. Sonja stays at the estate overnight on occasion, and Gwen commutes into the estate.

I was able to schedule a time with the ladies in June of 2018. The house is larger than it looks from the exterior. It's a white, Victorian frame house with a wraparound porch on two sides. Angel statues are placed all around the property. The house has three floors with multiple windows, and a second, front door on the side of the property.

Even walking upon the property, I felt like eyes were peering down on me. I stopped and looked up at each window, not really sure I wanted to see eyes or not.

Gwen opened the door, allowing me to enter. She spoke up first with her greeting. "Welcome to the 4th most terrifying house in Indiana."

The house was dark, not only with dark woodworking and dark curtains, but purposely kept dark.

At the dining room table sat Sonja, and I pulled out my chair. The three of us were seated in this room. The furniture isn't original, just furnishings to give the property atmosphere.

Gwen spoke up, "The house is alive. The house picks and chooses who volunteers here, who visits, who walks up the steps of the property. Even before people know it, the house decides what happens here."

Sonja nodded in agreement. "Contractors bail out. Workmen come to the house, and will give bids on repairs, but nobody ever returns to do the work. Phone calls aren't returned. Emails are ignored."

"What is it about the house, or is it the land?" I asked the ladies.

"Part of the concern is the land the house sits on. It does rest on limestone, and we know Indians were all over this part of the state. We do talk to the house. We do communicate with the ghosts here, on their time.

"At one time, the house was a boarding house. Many rooms were used. One family lived on the entire second floor.

"Before that, we know a doctor owned the house, and he later sold it to another doctor. We feel like in his practice, some of his patients passed away here.

"In 1925, Mable Hopper was laid to rest here.

"We know that Jessie Gibbon passed in 1934.

"This house is no stranger to death!" said Sonja.

I was eager to begin the investigation of the house. The ladies, who conduct the tours begin with the parlor. One of the ladies turned out the dining room chandelier to keep the house as dark as possible.

Something evil has attached itself to the two dolls displayed on the piano. Misfortune soon follows whomever handles the dolls.

Gwen shoved open the two pocket doors that led into the parlor. "Notice the charred, burned remains on the two doors and the frames. The house suffered a fire on Christmas," she said.

I looked at the doors and reached up rub the charred remains with my hand. I wanted to be able to touch a piece of the house's history.

"The family had adopted a little girl named Rachel.

"This happened in 1912. According to the story, Rachel was sneaking a peek of the presents under the Christmas tree. Rachel had gotten too close to the Christmas tree. At that time, candles were used light up the tree, and she had caught her dress on fire.

"The family was able to extinguish the burning Christmas tree. Since her adopted father was a doctor, Rachel was cared for at home.

"Rachel's bedroom was upstairs. Rachel didn't survive the fire. Due to her extreme burns, as a medical treatment, she was given morphine.

"Rachel died of an overdose of the morphine.

"She is one of the ghosts that haunt this house," said Sonja.

"Other strange things occur in this room," said Gwen.

"What do you mean?" I asked.

"Look at these two dolls on the upright piano. You don't want to touch them, if you can help it. Something menacing has attached itself to the two dolls.

"We know that people who have touched the dolls, moved them, held them in some capacity, well, let's say, all kinds of bad luck and bad circumstances soon happened.

"Equipment malfunctions. Machinery stops working. Batteries in cameras die. Car trouble, and some have even dealt with failed relationships after interacting with the two dolls," explained Gwen.

"It's almost like the two dolls are cursed!" I added. I didn't dare touch the dolls, I looked at them from a safe distance.

"Sometimes, I spend the night here and will sleep on this couch," said Sonja.

"You sleep here?" I asked almost surprised to hear.

"Yes, and on some nights, I'd wake up and hear growls in the room. Sometimes, something would yank off my blanket or I'd hear my name being called. On occasion, something would shout, 'wake up' to me.

"Sometimes I'd have weird dreams, or it would sound like someone would be in the next room coughing!

"One of the best things, the chandelier will move, and the prisms will tingle. Nobody would be upstairs, which might cause the chandelier to vibrate.

"We've had a lot of ghostly interactions in this room. Would you like to try to communicate with a spirt?" Gwen asked me.

I jumped at the chance, and eagerly answered yes. "What do you need to do first?"

Sonja turned out the lights in the room. She closed the charred pocket doors that led into the dining room. She crossed the room and pushed open the two pocket doors that separated the parlor from the main hallway and staircase. She got out two, small mag lights and positioned them on the stairs, with the lights facing up. Gwen and I sat down on the couch, the two mag lights were across the room, but facing us. Sonja sat down in a chair to our right. Due to the heavy curtains and the dark window shades designed to keep out any penetrating light, at that point, the room was in total darkness.

Stillness and quietness were in the room, until we could hear this thump, thump, drag sound, coming from the ceiling above. Even though the room was in total darkness, I turned and looked at Gwen, who was seated next to me. The sounds came again, as if something or someone was above us walking around.

"Something's here; it's moving around upstairs," said Sonja, "and we're alone in the house."

"Nobody is here, Robert, only the three of us." said Gwen.

Sonja gave the first direction, "If a ghost is with us, turn on one of the mag lights."

Our ghost was most cooperative. When asked to make the chandelier's sway and the prism's tingle, it happened!

Within seconds, one of the mag lights came on, followed by the second light. Two of the mag lights were shining right on my and Gwen's faces.

"Thank you, now turn out one of the lights," was the instruction given my Gwen.

Just as being told, one of the mag lights slowly dimmed and was turned out, yet the other remained on.

"Rachel, are you here, or are we being visited by someone else? If it is Rachel, turn on the light. If someone else is here, please turn out the other light," asked Gwen. The second light faded out, and all three of us were back in the darkness. I was invited to ask any type of a yes or no question of the spirit to get a response. Not being totally sure it wasn't Rachel; I asked a very general question.

"Did you die in the house? If yes, please turn on the light," was my question.

The mag lights on the dresser would turn on and off by themselves when asked simple yes and no questions.

Seconds passed. One light came on, followed by the second light. So, whoever was with us, did die in the house. Both lights were shining our way, which did cast strange shadows on the wall behind us.

Another thud sound was heard overhead. I saw Gwen look upwards at the ceiling, and I did, too. I noticed that Sonja was getting out her flashlight, one much larger that the two small, miniature mag lights.

Sonja turned on her flashlight and lit up the chandelier.

"Let us know you're with us, please cause the chandelier's prism to tinkle, or the chandelier to sway back and forth," Sonja asked of the ghost.

We didn't have to stare of the chandelier long until it gently started to sway, causing the dangling prisms to tinkle. I gasped, for I'd never seen anything like that happen on command like that.

Sonja turned out her flashlight, and the three of us continued to ask questions of the ghost. I never got a name or identity of the ghost that was responding to our questions, but it did turn the mag lights on and off as requested. After one question, we got no response at all, even after encouraging it to do something, either light up a mag light or cause the chandelier to sway and tinkle, but nothing else happened. After sitting in the dark parlor for a couple of minutes, we decided that the ghost had moved on, so we felt like it was time to explore elsewhere in the house. I was grateful that it used the mag lights to communicate with us, as well as some ghost making the chandelier tingle.

Sonja closed the two pocket doors that led into the hallway and Gwen, standing next to me, opened up the two charred pocket doors. We went into the dining room. To the left of the fireplace in the dining room, was a single door. Going through the room, we were led into what is now used as a bedroom.

"From what we understand, this room wasn't a bedroom at the time the family lived here. We believe it was an examination room for Dr. John, or possibly a waiting room. None of the furniture is original to the house at all. Some of the furniture has been donated and some has been purchased to look like period pieces. This particular room has on display some artifacts of bottles found, letters, and some personal items that have been returned to the estate," said Gwen.

Coins mysteriously would appear on objects in the house.

Gwen started telling me about some of the letters on display. I looked around and read some of the scripts. Sonja was on the opposite side of the room. I noticed she was setting up the two mag lights on the dresser. As we walked about the wooden floor, I could use hear the usual creaks from the wooden floor. Sonja was standing by the dresser and next to the bed, Gwen and I were in the back, near a window. Even though the three of us were standing still, there was still the sound of footsteps. Something was causing the old wooden floorboards to creak and groan from the weight of someone moving. I looked at Gwen and we looked at Sonja, still hearing the creaks on the floor. We weren't moving.

Sonja said, "Something followed us into the room. That's the creaking on the floor as if someone is walking."

"We're not moving," I mentioned to Gwen. "We're not making the creaking noises at all."

Sonja reached over and turned out the lamp on the dresser. The room was in total darkness now. I could hear the bed squeak as Sonja sat down. The two mag lights were in place. "Is someone with us? Please turn on the light so we'll know you're here," Sonja said.

It wasn't long, seconds actually, that the mag light came on. The beam of light shined on me.

"Is the doctor here?" I asked. "Turn the other light on, if the doctor is here."

The one light that was on, dimmed until it turned off.

The two ladies asked general questions, 'Are you happy here?': 'Did you die in the house?': 'Do you mind that we are visiting your place?': The lights came on, and with a negative answer, the lights went off. Sometimes, both lights would turn on and sometimes, both lights would go out.

After a few minutes, we were no longer getting any type of responses. Sonja was still seated on the bed, and Gwen and I were still in our positions where we first started communicating.

Plink, plink, was the sound that was heard. "What was that?" I asked.

"We find coins in this room, as well as in other rooms. Coins, just out of the blue, fall from the ceiling," said Gwen.

Sonja stood up and turned on the lamp. The three of us looking around on the furniture and the floor. I found two pennies and a nickel on the floor. Those coins were not on the floor where I was standing. I would have seen them, as often as we looked down at the floor as we heard creaking sounds.

"Those are nicknamed, 'coins from heaven' and they just appear in the room. If you'll look behind you, on the desk, are some of the coins we've found in here," said Gwen.

I turned around and on the top of the desk, several pennies, nickels, and dimes were scattered about. I placed the coins I'd found on the floor with the other coins. I lined the coins up in a row on the desk.

"Nails are found in here, and objects get thrown in this room," added Sonja.

Gwen walked across the room toward a closed door. "The bathroom is in here, and we believe it was used as an operating room."

"We've had investigators on the tour come running out of the bathroom, only to discover they have been scratched by something aggressive. Others have had nosebleeds for no reason. The medicine cabinet door just swings open on its own," added Sonja.

The beach balls would roll from the bed posts and onto the floor. The dolls on the bed will be moved into new configurations or repositioned or found elsewhere in the room.

I stepped inside of the bathroom. It has the traditional black and white tile print on the floor. I could see my reflection in the medicine cabinet mirror, and I feel like I gave it time to swing open the door, but it didn't happen.

Heading upstairs, we were provided with several more opportunities to do the investigations. Our first room was the room above the doctor's examination room on the first floor. This was Rachel's room. None of the furniture is original to this room of the house, but it is designed with bedroom furniture, dolls, and two inflated beach balls on the bed. I noticed on the dresser were several coins, and I spotted two pennies on the floor upon entering the room.

Gwen walked over to the dresser, and I noticed three of the exact same dolls were displayed.

"I purchased one of the dolls, just to make the room look more like a little girl's bedroom. Now here's what is so strange, almost puzzling. On that same day, two different visitors, or friends of the house, happened to drop by. The first lady gave me the exact, same doll. I thanked her, and she went on her way. Later that same day, another woman dropped by the house, and she wanted me to have this doll, which is the same doll! I looked at the doll, and realized, 'hey, I've got two more like it upstairs!' So, that's why you see three of the same dolls on the dresser. How do you think something like that could happen again?

"Now here's the real deal. Look at this burned doll.

On top of one of the dressers, was a burned, blackish charred doll that was in a small, tabletop curio case. The doll was standing upright in the case.

A psychic reported that a message was given to her, "This is what I looked like when I died!"

"When we were given the doll, we didn't think anything was more special about that doll than any other doll that we have in the room. It wasn't burned at all and looked like any little girl would pick it up and play with it.

"One evening, we were conducting a ghost investigation of the house. It was very late, and most people had already left for the night. The few of us who were here we were all standing in the dining room. Nobody was on the second floor.

"We heard this loud crash, as if something was thrown hard and it went tumbling down the stairs.

"We all rushed into the hallway and there at the bottom of the staircase, was this doll. However, this doll's appearance had changed dramatically at this point.

"The doll had a funny smell to it, and when we turned on the lights to see about was going on, that's when we noticed that the doll had been burned.

"It was in perfect condition upstairs! Now, the doll has been burned. "Nobody really wanted to touch it, so we just quickly passed it about the circle of us standing there.

"That particular group had a psychic with them.

"The psychic said she was starting to get a message, from the spirit of the doll.

"We looked at the psychic in anticipation. She closed her eyes and said that that message was from the little girl named Rachel.

"The psychic said in an almost, childlike voice, 'This is what I looked like when I died!" said Gwen.

That statement sent chills down my body! I wanted to touch the doll, just to see how it felt and maybe, have some connection with Rachel, but I didn't.

"We know that Rachel was badly burned in the fire at Christmas, and unfortunately, she died due to an overdose of morphine," said Gwen.

"Did Rachel's ghost toss the doll down the steps to get our attention? Is Rachel wanting to reaffirm her presence in the afterlife?

"So now, we keep the burned faced doll, which we've now named Rachel, in the glass curio cabinet. And there, she has remained," said Sonja.

Across the hall is the nursery of the house. It's a small room, with a concealed staircase leading to the attic of the house.

The nursery, being a small room, became quite crowed with the three of us in there.

"I never like to be alone in here," said Sonja.

"People have left this room with scratch marks on their arms and necks.

"The rocking chair will rock all by itself, too," added Gwen.

"We've also had visitors to the house report of being pushed on the staircase in the hallway.

"The attic steps are concealed in here, and the steps are very steep.

"We don't usually go upstairs, but what's happened with some frequency is that a male entity is up there. We don't know if it is human or not, but that last time I was up there, it said to me, 'Get out.'

"We have furniture upstairs, and it is large enough to be used as living space. The front room, we've named the Red Room, mostly because of the red furniture. The think the Red Room is more of the heart of the house. The bed in that room moves! We can be in the attic one day, and a few days later, go up there and the bed will be in another location, something pushes the bed!

"Visitors who are doing investigations have reported hearing sounds while upstairs too!"

I went upstairs to the attic and looked around. I saw the bed that does move on its own, but I didn't hear any animal noises. The two other ladies didn't go upstairs with me. I gingerly walked about, looking at the arrangement of the furniture, hoping I'd hear something. Unfortunately, I didn't stay too long. I was visiting in June, and on the third floor of the house, the heat up there was unbearable.

It was assumed that the servant's quarters were on the back side of the house on the second floor, but nobody knows for sure. This area has a back staircase that leads downstairs to the hallway near the kitchen, plus it has an exterior staircase for a private entrance or exit.

History of the house tells us that this area was once an apartment. We went into this area. It has a staircase in the center of the room, with a high railing to prevent anyone from falling over. Each side has an adjacent room.

We do know that one of the tenants took a serious fall in the bathroom. A gentleman fell while exiting the tub. In his fall, he landed in such a tragic way that he broke his neck and died there.

It's been reported by investigators that an apparition was seen, and it passed through a wall. Also, it's been said by investigators and my guides as well, that a voice has been heard, almost crying in pain, with the words of 'Help me.'

On one side of this back-upstairs apartment, is a large storage room with double doors. The pad lock is on the outside. Volunteers of the house have had to be rescued. A volunteer would go into this storage area and something would close the door and place the pad lock in place, locking the volunteer inside of the storage room! Thank goodness for the invention of cell phones, because the volunteer would have to call someone for help, or, follow the policy of a buddy system and never enter that storage room alone. Other volunteers have been scratched on the arms, neck, and legs, and have exited the storage room with red, deep marks.

Another volunteer and supporter of the house had mentioned that once, she was working in the upstairs apartment. She was alone in this area of the apartment, and not in the storage room. Something came up and pulled hard on her ponytail.

Another story that has been in circulation is that at one time, someone had been pushed over the shorter railing and fallen to their death. The railing that is in place today, is a railing that is in code for building and housing safety. This individual that was pushed over cashed through a more filmy, unstable and shorter railing.

An investigator who was monitoring this area stated in her notes of something with force, pushed her spirit box off of the seat of a chair. She also stated in her notes that an entity with red eyes and the shape of horns near its head made its presence known near that storage area.

Author's Note: At the end of the investigation, the two ladies asked if I'd ever participated in a tipping table session, and if so, would I like to do so. I'd only heard of tipping table sessions, but I'd never seen one nor did I know anyone who had participated. I was eager to give it a try.

In this case, the ladies said we'd use the upstairs hallway. We would open the doors to the rooms to allow any ghosts the opportunity to come forward and feel welcome. We set up the table there. The upstairs hallway was still fairly dark with the coverings and draperies over the windows.

We used a simple, maybe 14-inch diameter round table with three detachable legs. Gwen screwed the three legs into the bottom of the round table. Sonja found three chairs.

"To make this work, we must place our hands on the table. Our pinky fingers and thumbs must touch and remain connected as long as possible. This position will form a circle. Whatever the table does, such as moves, jumps up, rises up, turns, tips, tilts, try not to release your fingers and follow the table. If the table turns in a rotation, stand up and follow the table.

"We'll communicate with a spirit and ask it yes or no questions to start with. We'll tell the table to respond by tipping.

"Be prepared for anything to happen with the table," said Gwen.

The three of us placed out hands on the table and touched thumbs and pinky fingers, encircling the table. A prayer of protection was offered up, for angels to wrap loving arms around us with a shield and for no harm to come our way during the session, or afterwards.

Sonja started out the session by inviting a ghost to join us, any ghost in the house was welcome. She asked the ghost to make its presence known by either making a knocking sound, or to causing the table to rise.

A knocking sound was heard in the hallway, just over Sonja's shoulder. The table did vibrate a little after we heard the knocks.

The first question was asked that would have required a yes or no answer. The ghost was told to push the table one direction, into Gwen's lap for yes, and onto my lap for a no answer.

This was a simple question, just asking if someone was with us and if you (the ghost) would want to communicate with us.

The table was pushed onto Gwen's lap for the yes answer.

Several more questions were asked of the visiting ghost. Early in the session, Sonja said she'd recite the alphabet, that way, we could get a name of this ghost. The ghost was told to push the table onto my lap when the letter was used in its name. Nothing happened until the letter F was spoken. That caused the table to be shoved onto my lap. She continued until she reached the letter R, and the table again, was shoved onto my lap. We pieced out some other letters to reveal a name, that identified itself as being a distant relative of mine, not a ghost of the house.

We transitioned from general house questions for any ghost that was present, to being more personal, more specific questions that would pertain to me.

The table became much more active. It did rise up, even to the point of where we had to stand up as the table would rise.

On several occasions, the table tilted upwards and was on my lap, even to the point where I had to scoot back my chair. I could almost sense something pushing the table onto my lap. The table had weight to it.

Each time after an intense session, the three of us would stop and reposition the table back onto the floor, relax our hands and fingers, and then, place them back onto the table.

One time a question was asked, and the table rotated to the point all three of us were leaning, almost to the point of having to change chairs to follow the table.

The table did rise up and land hard on the floor to some of the questions and comments that were made. Apparently, something really agreed with what was said, or wanted its opinion of displeasure known. Sometimes, the table responded to our conversation with movement and not to a direct yes or no question.

It was true, it did seem like the table had a mind of its own!

I realize the passages written here are vague to the reader. Keep in mind, once the table tipping session began, most of the questions were directed toward me with the ghost that we were in communication with. The questions asked were more of a personal nature about my family, health, finances and future, so for confidentially, I'd prefer not to state the specific questions or share what was revealed. It's anyone's guess as to whether the events detailed here will come to pass or not.

After a few minutes to silence and no table tipping activity, we released our hands from the table and relaxed our fingers. Each of us, seemed to take a deep sigh of relief and a breath. It takes a minute or two to process what happened and to reflect on what was said.

I thought, you as the reader might find it interesting to know about a tipping table session and what might happen if the opportunity ever did arise and you decided to participate.

Whose Furniture Is It, Anyway, in the Seelbach Hotel

A very grand hotel for the living, and the deceased.

Back in June of 2017, I had a ghostly sighting, and not only a sighting, but it spoke to me.

During my ghost walking tour season, on Friday and Saturday nights, I always make it a practice to stop by the Seelbach Hotel. One thing, I like to see if my area that I use is available. On some occasions, the hotel has an event in progress in the area that I like to use for my guests and my presentation. I also, use this as time to arrange the furniture into a large circle, that way, once I arrive with my guests, the chairs are arranged. The guests can be seated, and I can begin right away once everyone gets comfortable.

On one summer night of 2017, I was on the mezzanine area of the hotel. I had just begun my usual routine of pulling and pushing chairs and forming a large circle. I was the only person on the mezzanine area, and I had a clear line of vision, in case anyone ascending the main staircase or if anyone was moving toward the Oak Room Restaurant. I was alone in this area, or least I thought I was alone.

I had just repositioned one of the chairs, when I stopped short and heard a man's voice. His presence just about startled me, since I didn't see anyone walking my way. I would have seen that individual.

"Do you not like how we have our furniture arranged? "a demanding voice caught my attention.

There, before my eyes, stood a gentleman with heavy facial features. He had white hair, parted on the side, and a very thick, brushy like mustache across his face. His clothing was of another time period, definitely not how men would dress today. I did notice he had on a heavy, woolen looking sport coat in the brown color, with one button buttoned across his chest. His trousers were dark, and he was wearing a white colored shirt with a dark colored necktie. He was a short, portly fellow, who spoke to me in a deep voice.

Thinking back, what caused me to stop in my tracks were the haunting words of how he emphasized the words 'we' and 'our' as if he had ownership here. He didn't strike me as being just a hotel guest who wondered over to make conversation with me about what I was doing; but no, it was as if he had authority to inquiry of my actions.

Now, people who are guests of the hotel, do ask me what I'm doing, and I politely tell them that I'll be doing a ghost walk program in the area shortly. Being a good businessman and knowing that the folks who are asking most likely are hotel guests, I do invite them to drop by. Some do, and some I never see again, but I do consider it to be an act of courtesy.

I tugged on the chair just an inch or so and looked up to respond to the gentleman who spoke to me. However, with just a blink of the eye, I looked up and he was gone. Vanished! Nobody was standing there.

I moved away from the chair and raced over to the balcony railing that is just above the main staircase. I looked down, expecting to the white-haired gentleman descending the staircase, but nobody was there!

From my vantage point by the balcony railing, all I had to do was turn my head to the left. I had a clear view of the anteroom and then, a clear shot into the Oak Room Restaurant. Nobody was in sight.

Where could he have gone to so suddenly? It was almost if the man had simply vanished into thin air.

I slowly walked about the mezzanine area, just hoping for something, some sign, or something that I had overlooked, and then realized, there he is. But my efforts were no more than a waste of time.

I returned to positioning the chairs into a large circle for my guests, but in the back of my mind, I kept thinking about the gentleman who appeared out of thin air and spoke to me in such an authoritative voice. I wasn't quite ready yet to think of the gentleman as being a ghost.

The presence of that gentleman remained with me for several more weeks. Each Friday and Saturday nights, I'd be in the Seelbach, and I'd walk around and look for the gentleman. I tried to reason to myself, that he must have been an employee, one that I'd never met; but each time, I never saw anyone who fit the description.

I knew to help solve this mystery, I needed to speak with my friend, Mr. Rhodes, the head security guard of the hotel. I'd worked and interviewed with Mr. Rhodes before, and he is a believer in ghost. I knew he would be my best contact.

A couple weeks had passed until I'd made it downtown on a weekend night to speak with Mr. Rhodes.

I had the front desk call for Mr. Rhodes, and mentioned that this was a social call, and that nothing was wrong. Mr. Rhodes was glad to see me in the lobby. We shook hands and chatted a bit, and then I wanted to share with him my experience.

"I've got a ghost story to share with you, and I want to take you to the location where it happened," I told him. The two of us climbed up the staircase and stood on the mezzanine level. I could tell that Mr. Rhodes was eager to hear of my experience.

"This is where it happened to me, back in the early summer," I said.

I shared with him the exact story, and I even moved about, and repositioned a chair, just as I had done on that night. I pointed out to Mr. Rhodes, that this is where the ghost of the gentleman appeared.

Even as I spoke, Mr. Rhodes was just about able to chime in and add to my description of the ghostly gentleman.

After my detailed explanation, Mr. Rhodes asked me, "Do you remember when the hotel decided to remodel the old Otto's Restaurant and transform it into Gatsby's on 4th?"

I nodded in agreement, yes, I do remember that remodeling project.

"One morning, I came into work and two construction workers wanted to speak with me. I didn't know what it was about, and unfortunately, I feared the worst, that something had happened.

"The two men were still a little shaken about what they had seen. One man told me, that they were in early, back in the construction site, just getting set up.

"They were the only folks around. It was still dark outside, and only a few lights were on in the restaurant.

"All of a sudden, the two men looked up, and there stood and older man, lots of white hair, with a thick mustache.

"He was wearing some older clothing, and they noted that he had on brown colored sport coat, a white shirt, and a tie.

"The men said that he was just standing there, giving them this glare, almost a look of disgust.

"He said to them, 'The Seelbach brothers aren't happy, and this restaurant will be cursed!'

"If that wasn't frightening enough, then he just disappeared, right before their eyes!

"He was gone. Well, the two men just looked at each other, and made some jokes about how early it was, and their eyes were playing tricks on them.

"The more they talked about it, and the more they looked around for where he came from, and where did he go? Of course, they couldn't find anything evidence whatsoever so.

"The mystery still remains. The guys never could come up with anything.

"Now here we are, a couple years later, and you're telling me about seeing this older, white-hair gentleman here on the mezzanine," Mr. Rhodes said.

Mr. Rhodes and I went down to a historical display that the hotel has set up in the back lobby. Some pictures of the two Seelbach brother, along with china, menus, room keys, and other memorabilia are on display.

Mr. Rhodes and I kicked around some possibilities of what the gentleman had said to me, and what he said to the two construction workers.

I studied the photos and made some connections to the gentleman that I saw, and the photos of the Seelbach brothers.

I was trying to analyze what was said and how he emphasized the words 'we' and 'our' as if he had some ownership of the property.

And adding to this reference to the brothers, weren't happy, I come up with this theory.

I know for a fact that the two-large chandeliers that hang in the main lobby aren't original to the hotel. The two chandeliers came from the Phoenix Hotel, which was Charlie Seelbach's hotel. Charlie owned the Phoenix Hotel in Lexington, Kentucky. The Phoenix was demolished for the construction of UK's Rupp Arena. Thank goodness, someone had enough foresight to bring the two chandeliers from the Phoenix and hang them in the lobby here.

When the chandeliers came, did the ghost of Charlie Seelbach come with them? Does Charlie still roam the halls of the Seelbach, keeping a watchful eye on anything thing new or improvements being made at the hotel?

Does Charlie communicate with the two brothers, Otto and Louis Seelbach? And did he really have confirmation from the two brothers, that they weren't happy with the closure of Otto's Restaurant and the new and improved, Gatsby's on 4th? Was the newer venue for dining, really cursed?

About Louisville Ghost Walks

Louisville Ghost Walks is in its 15 year of telling thrilling ghost stories of the city's most famous addresses. Guests from across the United States and foreign countries have joined Mr. Ghost Walker to hear the stories of hauntings, murder, and mystery on this 90-minute tour.

Louisville Ghost Walks welcomes all guests. Some guests believe in the paranormal while others are just curious about the supernatural and want to learn and hear more of the hauntings. Each guest leaves with something to reflect upon, whether it be a memory of a haunting in a building, an eerie crime location, or a chuckle from one on the night's humous story.

Louisville Ghost Walks encourages guests, who have a story to share, to be sure to tell it. I'm always ready to listen and find out more about what guests have experienced, it here or far away. Ghosts and their stories are found in all locations of the world and in all cultures. Someone always has a story to tell, insight, or a chilling experience just waiting to be told.

I do wish each guest a pleasant night and safe drive home. I like to leave with them this lasting thought, that as they look in their rear-view mirror from the driver's seat of their automobile, that they might just see an ashen pale, hollowed out face staring back at them. Remember, ghosts can follow you home!

If you'd like to enjoy a 90-minute ghost walking tour, the schedule begins with the second weekend of May and continues until the second weekend of November. The tales are told on Friday and Saturday nights.

Contact: 502-689-5117

LouGhstWalks@aol.com

LouisvilleGhostWalks.com

Books

Welcome, and I hope you have enjoyed reading *Haunted Louisville 4: Dark Screams and Troubling Tales*. Are you wanting to read more in this series? As with all of my books in the Haunted Louisville series, I hope that at the end of the book, you'll have plenty to think about, reflect upon, and pause as you think about that the noise you heard, the cold feeling you just experienced, and the dark shadow that flashed before your eye, is more than just your imagination. Maybe something has decided to join you on the evening, maybe something has decided to follow you home, and maybe something just wants to keep you company. Could it be ghostly? Only you can decide upon that!

The other books in the series include:

- *Haunted Louisville: History and Hauntings from the Derby City*
- *Haunted Louisville 2: Beyond Downtown, More Hauntings from the Derby City*
- *Haunted Louisville 3: You Are Never Alone*

About the Author

Robert Parker, author of the three previous Haunted Louisville series of books, has just completed his fourth book, Haunted Louisville 4...Dark Screams from Troubling Tales. The stories in his fourth book include some of his personal experiences on investigations for the reader, which some tales are local, and some others have occurred in other states. Robert enjoys the interviews and meeting new people who have had ghostly encounters who are willing to share with him their stories. Robert owns Louisville Ghost Walks, a ghost walking tour with over 13 years of storytelling experiences of the downtown streets.

Robert is currently employed as a middle school social studies teacher in the Jefferson County Public Schools system. His students enjoy hearing his stories being told, with their responses of 'ohh and ahh' of each scary detail and with the wide-eyed excitement of one of the oldest forms of entertainment, storytelling is presented. Students make the best audiences around!

He is also part of the downtown community as an activist for dealing with the homeless population in the city and trying to meet their basic needs. He has invested time and his resources in the two homeless shelters of the city, Hotel Louisville and Wayside Christian Mission. Robert will be concluding his teaching career within Jefferson County Public Schools as a middle school teacher very soon. Robert plans to continue being involved in the education system, with possible opportunities to provide instruction with the GED program to help others who didn't complete their high school graduation requirements. Robert enjoys traveling to neighboring cities to discover ghostly activities and opportunities for interviews or research. Don't be surprised to find

Robert exploring an older, abandoned building, or climbing to the top of a historical church's bell tower, or tasting local foods found at the popular restaurants.

AMERICAN HAUNTINGS INK

For more books about history. Hauntings. Crime and the unexplained, check out the selection from the publisher of the *Haunted Louisville* books, American Hauntings Ink.

www.americanhauntingsink.com